Southwest

THREE PEOPLES IN GEOGRAPHICAL

CHANGE, 1600-1970

SOUTHWEST

D. W. Meinig

NEW YORK
OXFORD UNIVERSITY PRESS
LONDON 1971 TORONTO

FOREWORD

Southwest is one of two books by which Oxford University Press is initiating a series of succinct but, we trust, stimulating volumes in a little cultivated field of American historical scholarship—that which is usually called historical geography or geographical history. We prefer to think of them as studies of changing geography or of geographical change. Those of us engaged in the enterprise are, for the most part, professional geographers and, although our major readership must be among historians, and it is to them that we mainly address ourselves, our central and vital concern with place, location, and interaction or diffusion through space clearly identifies us in our own profession. But we are writing for all social scientists and humanists as well, and, we hope, for a general literate public, too.

The other volume is David Ward's *Cities and Immigrants: A Geography of Change in Nineteenth Century America,* which analyzes the changing urban geography of the country, much of it concentrated on the diametrically opposite section of the country, the northeast, in the nineteenth century. Other studies soon to join these two include a double volume on the historical geography of Canada, and separate treatments of colonial New England and the colonial southern seaboard. These we expect to be followed by studies of the middle colonies, the first trans-Appalachian expansion, the ante-bellum Midwest, the Gulf South, a new interpretation of the Great Plains, and special studies of California and the Pacific Northwest. Our ultimate hope is to supply a small library of thematic studies of different places and times in our continental development that can serve as joint or supplemental texts for college and university courses in history and geography. We will miss our mark, however, if each volume does not provide something of a new interpretive adventure.

Donald William Meinig is rapidly emerging as one of the most evocative interpreters of the evolution of the American West. The present volume follows on the appearance of the comprehensive, prize-winning *The Great Columbia Plain*, in 1968, and *Imperial Texas*, a most satisfying vignette of that colorful commonwealth, in 1969. Now chairman of one of our major graduate departments of geography at Syracuse University, Meinig comes originally out of the Pacific Northwest and earned his doctorate at the University of Washington. For many years he taught at the University of Utah in Salt Lake City and while there became fascinated by the Mormon adventure. His paper on "The Mormon Culture Region" in the *Annals of the Association of American Geographers,* 55 (1965) 91-220, has been called a landmark in the study of the historical cultural geography of the United States. That he is by no means parochial in his interests is evident in his *On the Margins of the Good Earth: The South Australian Wheat Frontier, 1869–1884,* 1962 (No. 2 in the Monograph Series of the Association of American Geographers), and in his lively historical contributions to John H. Thompson, ed. *Geography of New York State,* 1966.

Meinig's study of the Southwest effectively captures the atmosphere of this most exotic of our national regions as its geography of occupation and resource use has changed over nearly four centuries. It is a book about peoples, chiefly of three contending groups: the Indians who wouldn't go away, the Hispanos whose ancestors have shared it with the Indians for most of the four hundred years, and the Anglos whose presence now extends over a sesquicentury. But it is always a study of peoples in place: cultures and economies share top billing with the desert earth, the piñon and pine-clad hills and mountains, and the swirling exotic rivers tamed to water broad acres amid the sun, the dust, the cactus, and the salt bush of the bolsons and plains. It was in 1912 that Arizona and New Mexico became states and, as they approach their diamond jubilees in 1972, it seems appropriate that a sympathetic but honest and toughly analytical study of this kind should precede the great precipitation of sentimentality about the Southwest to which we shall certainly be subjected. This volume should supplement any and all historical studies of the region.

ANDREW H. CLARK

Madison, Wisconsin
December 1970

PREFACE

This book attempts a fresh look at a famous and oft-studied area. In detail it contains little that is new—each topic has its literature, and on some subjects, such as Indian cultures, frontier conquest, or the "new Southwest," this literature is large and varied. What is new is the way in which these topics and many others are put together to form a coherent picture of regional change. As a geography, that picture is ordered in terms of place and is complete in its coverage of area. This emphasis upon places and a consistent concern for areal relationships make such a work a complement to the more standard regional histories. Similarly, the historical structure of the work and its emphasis upon the changing areal relationships of the several distinct social groups, rather than upon contemporary patterns and problems of man and his use of the land make it a complement to standard American regional geographies.

The picture displayed by so small a book on so large and complex a region can be no more than a rather crude panorama. I only hope that the over-all effect suggests a type of interpretation which other students of this region, and of American regionalism more generally, will consider useful, and that the more detailed pattern, limited as it is, will suggest a number of themes well worth elaboration at different scales. Certainly the student of social geography, whether he is more interested in specific spatial and ecological examples or in general models of structure and behavior, will find the Southwest rich ground for study.

The several peoples which are so central to the themes of this overview have been little more than denoted as distinct cultures or subcultures, but the bibliography lists a number of studies which offer extensive descriptions of one or more. As for the "three peoples" in the subtitle, it is perhaps not inappropriate at this point to assure the reader that I have tried both to show how the generality of three is in detail more nearly a dozen, and yet to suggest also how the collective terms "Indian," "Hispano," and "Anglo" have long been appropriate in certain contexts of study and, more important, increasingly represent a basic frame of reference in the minds of Southwestern peoples themselves.

This work is part of a larger study in progress in which I have tried to interpret the historical development and special character of the American West as being grounded in a series of more or less discrete, in places sharply contrasting, and in some degree competitive, socio-cultural regions. It is thus a companion to "The Mormon Culture Region" and *Imperial Texas.* I am very pleased indeed to have *Southwest* issued as part of a still broader series of interpretive studies of the historical geography of Canada and the United States being developed under the guiding hand of Andrew H. Clark. I have had the benefit of Professor Clark's sharp editorial eye before, and his suggestions for improvement of this manuscript have only deepened an already great indebtedness which has accrued from many years of practical help, general encouragement, and inspiration.

I thank the John Simon Guggenheim Memorial Foundation and Syracuse University for generous grants which made possible the library research, field reconnaissance, and preparation of the manuscript. I also wish to thank Professor George McCleary for his skilled work on the maps, which are such a critical part of a study of this kind.

D. W. MEINIG

Syracuse, New York
December 1970

CONTENTS

FIGURES

TABLES

Southwest

1 THE SOUTHWEST: A DEFINITION

The Southwest is a distinctive place to the American mind but a somewhat blurred place on American maps, which is to say that everyone knows that there is a Southwest but there is little agreement as to just where it is. Some would write it so broadly across the continent from the Pacific Ocean to the Gulf of Mexico as to include Nevada, Utah. Colorado, and Oklahoma as well as California, Texas, and the states directly between, a full quarter or more of the entire nation. Others would define it more narrowly, but still with little general agreement as to its proper bounds. It is thus incumbent upon those who use the term to offer a clear definition and rationale at the outset. That such regional delineations should emanate from the purpose of the study is axiomatic.

If in a work of social geography we might logically begin by making our definition dependent upon the presence of certain peoples, we are quickly brought into at least general focus upon a particular region. The term "Southwest" is of course an ethnocentric one: what is south and west to the Anglo-American was long the north of the Hispano-American, and the overlap of the colonizing thrusts of these two continental invaders—the one approaching west from the Atlantic Seaboard, the other north from central Mexico—suggests a first element in the definition of a distinctive cultural border zone. Whether based upon the historic patterns of the several specific thrusts of the Spanish and Mexicans or the presence in significant numbers today of Spanish-Americans, that zone is an extensive one, reaching from the vicinity of San Francisco Bay to Galveston Bay. (Fig. 1-1) But if we add the continued presence of the Amer-

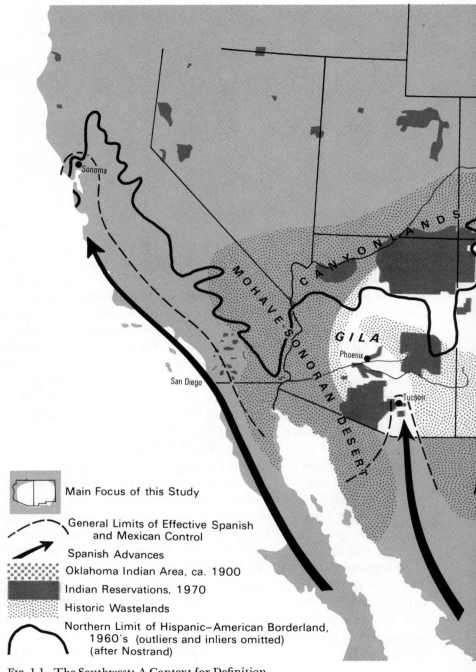

Main Focus of this Study

General Limits of Effective Spanish
  and Mexican Control

Spanish Advances

Oklahoma Indian Area, ca. 1900

Indian Reservations, 1970

Historic Wastelands

Northern Limit of Hispanic–American Borderland,
  1960's (outliers and inliers omitted)
  (after Nostrand)

FIG. 1-1. The Southwest: A Context for Definition

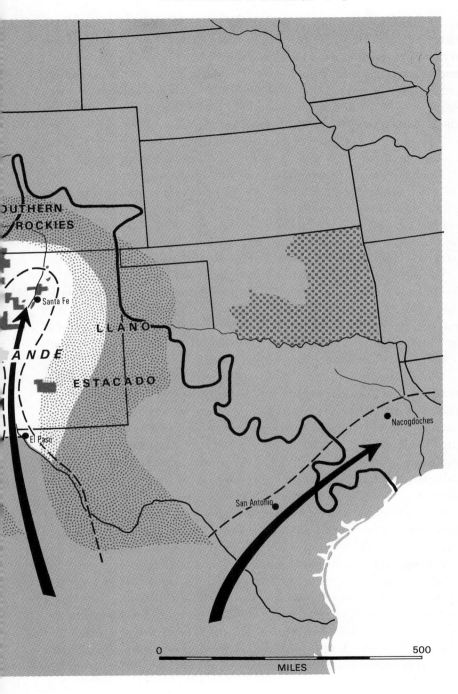

SOUTHERN
ROCKIES

Santa Fe

LLANO

ANDE

ESTACADO

El Paso

Nacogdoches

San Antonio

0   500

MILES

ican Indians as a significant part of the regional scene, our concern is narrowed from the whole breadth of these Anglo-Hispanic borderlands to that portion lying between Texas and California, for neither of these famous states has more than few tiny reservations and a very few Indians remaining. The major non-reservation Indian area in Oklahoma lies well beyond the Hispanic zone and is quite separated in position and in specific Indian cultures from New Mexico and Arizona.

The physical character of the area thus defined by the general juxtaposition of these three peoples is by no means uniform, though it is dominated by mountain-and-bolson or high plateau country and a relatively dry climate. More significant to the search for a workable regional definition is the fact that it has tended to be set apart on the west, north, and east by broad zones of difficult country—the Mohave-Sonoran Desert, the Colorado River canyonlands, the Southern Rockies, and the Llano Estacado—lands which long were and mostly still are thinly populated.

On the south the international boundary, now more than a century old, and antedating many of the major population movements and settlement developments, is so decisive to all modern relationships that it may be taken as a precise edge even though it cuts directly across the grain of the country and severs some of the Indians and Hispanos from their cultural kin and older connections further south.

During the American era the development of California and Texas on either side as two areas strongly self-conscious of being, and widely acknowledged to be, very distinct parts of the nation has tended to accentuate the separateness of the area in between, just as Mormon-dominated Utah and, in a much vaguer way, the common image of mountainous Colorado have helped to define a regional border along the north. Such patterns have been strongly reinforced in modern times by the emergence of metropolitan "fields." Thus as measured by basic metropolitan services, such as newspapers, banking, and wholesaling, the combined reach of Los Angeles, Salt Lake City, Denver, and the several large Texas cities leaves a large area in between served by its own centers.

But although this Anglo-Hispano-Indian combination of peoples living within this rather detached area defines the Southwest as a general region relevant to our purpose, it is also apparent that within those gross bounds there has been relatively little close unity in developments and the area has never had a single focus. Historical movements, though often quite parallel in kind, have tended to be fixed in two quite distinct areas which, if in some ways similar in character, are not only distant from one another but have been separated by formidable barriers. Each of these nuclear areas is served by a major stream, the Rio Grande on the one hand, the Gila on the other; each is the home of agricultural Indians; and each was a salient of the Spanish frontier, but the two were separated through several centuries by the Apache-held highlands in between. The Anglos were the first to initiate any significant moves to bind these parts together but they never succeeded in making it a cohesive whole. While many Anglo developments have given the area some greater integrity as a region, other actions and consequences, most notably the political definition of an Arizona and a New Mexico and the rise of the metropolitan centers of Albuquerque and El Paso along the Rio Grande and Phoenix and Tucson in the Gila Basin, have powerfully reinforced this historic dualism.

The establishment of these political boundaries has further complicated the problem of regional definition, for although Arizona and New Mexico encompass in general not only the two main historically nuclear areas but the wider areas ultimately developed by extensions from them, they do not delimit such areas precisely, embracing rather more in some sectors and less in others. The largest anomaly is along the eastern border where the New Mexican boundary includes the western margins of the Great Plains, areas eventually colonized and developed by contiguous expansions westward from Kansas and Texas rather than eastward from the Rio Grande Valley. We cannot, however, simply exclude that area from our concern, for despite a different heritage and combination of peoples, it profoundly affects the social relations and balance of power within the state as a whole. An equally important but smaller discordance lies just to the south, where the western promontory of Texas extends to the El Paso district, an area historically and currently more closely bound to the Southwest as here defined than to its political unit. Some lesser discordances along the northern border will be noted later.

The Southwest thus defined—in general, Arizona, New Mexico, and the El Paso district—despite a persistent dualism and more internal diversity and less focus than such a single term suggests, has nevertheless a sufficiently common set of people and problems enmeshed in a common heritage and is sufficiently set apart by physical and cultural differences from its neighbors to make it a reasonable regional unit for the purpose and scale of this interpretation. It has the further merit of conforming rather closely with the view of many of its own residents. For as Oliver La Farge, a highly qualified regional interpreter, has noted:

> If you ask a New Mexican what constitutes the Southwest, he will name
> New Mexico and Arizona; after hesitation, he may add the adjacent por-
> tions of Colorado, Utah and Nevada. California, Texas, and Oklahoma
> he rejects. . . (La Farge, p. 216)

That suggests a basic area, an ambiguous border zone on the north and
a distinct separation on the east and west. It seems evident that most any
Arizonan would offer a similar view.

Why there is such a "Southwest" in the minds of such people should
become clear from the chapters that follow.

2 THE SPANISH ERA:

1598-1820's

The Spanish conquered the upper Rio Grande country almost four hundred years ago, ruled it for well over two hundred years, and then, a century and a half ago, were ousted. Not only some general results of that era but some of the very patterns of its opening years are still a vivid part of the social geography of the region. That this should be so, in contrast with the results of European-Indian contacts so common elsewhere in the continent, arises from the special character of the peoples involved: the fact that an important body of the Indians were village agricultural societies, and that their conquerors sought as a major goal to control the Indians as a resource rather than remove them as an encumbrance. Thus despite the very great harshness of the Spanish intrusion and the gross deformations it wrought in geography, demography, and culture, major remnants of the sixteenth-century Indian pattern are still a basic part of the twentieth-century scene.

The Spanish found the Pueblo Indians occupying sites along and near the Rio Grande for nearly two hundred miles: from Senecu on the south at the edge of the long desert, to Taos on the north at the foot of the highest ranges. (Fig. 2-1) To the east, beyond the mountains bordering the river, was a parallel but less continuous string of others: from Gran Quivira (to use the present name of its ruins) to the Manzano and Galisteo pueblos to Pecos, the great outpost along the river of that name guarding the passageway to the Plains. To the west of the Rio Grande the pattern was quite different: widely separated clusters of villages built close upon the flank or upon the very top of some bold mesa—Acoma,

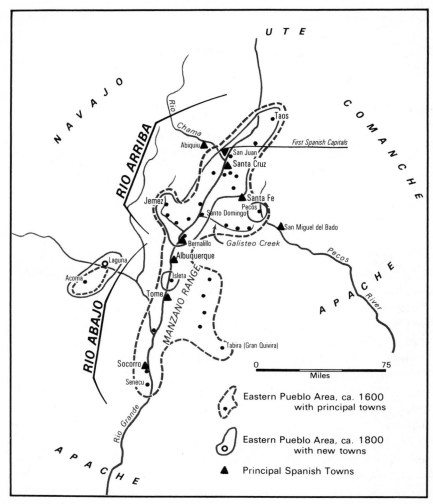

FIG. 2-1. The Pueblos and the Spanish

Zuñi, and the Hopi villages—in site, structure, and general situation more like their ancestral cliff dwellings in the recesses of the canyonlands to the north than those on the valley floors of their kin to the east.

There were perhaps forty thousand Indians in the four or five dozen villages of the Rio Grande area and another six or seven thousand in the isolated pueblos on the western mesas. Each village was a compact mass of rectangular, flat-roofed, and contiguous houses of adobe or adobe-covered stone, in some places terraced one upon another two, three, or more stories, the whole creation a great drab pile so completely formed of and blended with its surroundings that from a distance it might appear to be more like an intricate angular carving from a great earthen mound than a laborious construction of mud, wood, and stone. Each village contained several hundred people, the largest two thousand or more, and each was remarkably autonomous, self-contained in society and economy, living from its own nearby irrigated fields, in some contact with, but largely independent of, neighboring villages. Despite a generally common culture this Pueblo region was sharply compartmentalized into several distinct language areas each with further dialectal differences within. There was no inter-pueblo organization, no common council, no capital, and thus the Pueblo country was a region of similar parts which did not function as a whole.

The distinctiveness of the region was greatly heightened by the fact that these Pueblos were surrounded by the Apaches, Indians of a very different culture who were spread thinly in many small bands over the extensive plains, plateaus, and mountains, and who lived by hunting and gathering, trading and raiding. They had no really permanent villages and their territorial patterns were rather fluid; their relationships with the Pueblos were rather fragile, sustained by the exchange of the products of the hunt for those of the field, but sporadically broken by robbery and war.

The Spanish conquest and control of this Upper Rio Grande country was a remarkable movement by any comparison. Although something of the area and its people had been known since Coronado's return in 1542, the Oñate expedition of 1598 represented a sudden extension of Spanish colonization seven hundred miles beyond the Santa Barbara mines, the northernmost Spanish settlements on the Mexican Plateau at the time. It was a direct thrust with a set purpose: an abrupt annexation of the whole of the Pueblo country from the Hopi areas to those of the Pecos, the superimposition of Spanish military, civil, and ecclesiastical control, and the colonization of available lands by Spanish settlers.

The ponderous party which came upriver that first year, with its eighty-three wagons, hundreds of men, and thousands of cattle, had ample force and supplies to initiate the task, and in so doing they necessarily began to reshape the human geography of the region. Oñate's early capitals (San Juan de los Caballeros and Villa de San Gabriel) at the mouth of the Chama were soon considered to be too far north and too near to established pueblos to be the most efficient site for the government, and thus a decade later La Villa Real de la Santa Fe de San Francisco was laid out thirty miles to the south along a small unused stream at the edge of the mountains—a site more pivotal to the main frontiers of the north at Taos, Pecos, Galisteo, and Jemez, and sufficiently more central as to give rise to "Rio Arriba" and "Rio Abajo" as common designations for the country above and below the capital area. Meanwhile the missionaries had established their headquarters at Santo Domingo, one of the largest pueblos and one more nearly midway along the main axis. Over the years a network of missons, presidios, towns, new farm villages, and ranches was developed. By means of their own labors, the recruited or forced labors of the Indians, the extraction of tribute from each pueblo, and trade with the nomads, some wealth was wrenched from this hard and distant frontier. Thus the great caravans which every two or three years brought in the supplies necessary for the missionary, military, and civil work took sheep, wool, hides, pine nuts, blankets, and occasionally slaves back to Mexico. Such traffic, following Oñate's route, provided the only regular link with the outside world, although the distance to civilization was shortened by two hundred miles in the eighteenth century with the development of Chihuahua as the metropolis of the northern frontier.

But the Spanish never had the manpower, skills, or resources fully to accomplish their task and their tenure was always uneasy and hazardous. They never established any sustained control over the western pueblos and in one unique concerted Pueblo uprising in 1680 they were driven completely from the upper Rio Grande with heavy losses. It took sixteen years for them to restore their grip, and ever after they were faced with at least passive resistance and at times local revolts: an abrasive relationship between an invincible invader and an indomitable people which eased but never ended through all their years.

Two centuries of such a troubled history took a heavy toll. Rebellions and retaliations, forced removals and refugee movements, plus the ravages of disease and drought and attacks on every side from the nomadic tribes quite radically altered many of the earlier patterns. By the early 1800's the main Pueblo region was hardly half as long or half as wide as it had been in 1600. Every village but one along the eastern front had been abandoned, first the Manzano, then the Galisteo pueblos, leaving only a few score people, a remnant from wars and epidemics, at once-great Pecos. For the rest, the Indians had gradually withdrawn from the edge of the plains to the greater security of the valley in the face of re-

peated attacks, especially from the Comanches, who, spreading southward during these years, now dominated all this eastern borderland. The
rebellion of 1680 had abruptly disrupted the old and also created a new
settlement area. All the pueblos south of Isleta were abandoned, but Christian Indians fleeing with the Spanish established a new oasis just downriver from the mission and river-crossing on the Chihuahua trail at Paso
del Norte, where the names of some of their first villages still exhibit
their upriver antecedents: Isleta del Sur, Socorro del Sur. (Fig. 2-1) Over
the years many other pueblos were abandoned under less dramatic cir-
cumstances and only one new one, Laguna, near Acoma, was founded.
Thus in the 1800's the main Pueblo region extended only from Taos to
Sandia, with Isleta now rather apart below: nineteen villages remaining
of the more than sixty originally captured by the Spanish. Acoma,
Zuñi, and the Hopi settlements were also much reduced in strength.
Altogether there were probably no more than 8000 Pueblo Indians, only
a sixth of the sixteenth-century population. Nevertheless, even though
heavily reduced in number, contracted in area, and inevitably altered
in culture, the Pueblos maintained a remarkable integrity as a people.
Within the village walls their social cohesion was unbroken and their
own language and customs persisted. Although the Catholic Church was
a prominent part of the visible scene, it was rarely central either in location or allegiance, in some villages nominally accepted, in others largely
ignored, in all at most no more than co-existing with the *kiva* and the
ancient rituals.

There were of course more fully Christian Indians outside the pueblos, whole villages of them in some places, as, most prominently, in the
El Paso oasis. Although there was a strong tendency for such people to
become more Spanish in other ways as well, wherever they were congre-
gated and isolated they long persisted as basically Indian societies. But
such groups were very minor compared with the most general product
of contact, for two peoples so long together as the Spanish and the Indians had created a third, a blend in blood as well as culture. Soldier
settlements alongside Indian pueblos, the extensive use of Indian labor
in homes and towns, growing numbers of captives and slaves from the
nomadic bands, from these and other practices, from formal marriages
and casual contacts, came the *mestizo* population. Although usually
largely (and often almost wholly) Indian in blood they became increasingly Spanish in culture—in language and religion, behavior and attire—
cultivating their fields in ancient ways but also raising cattle and sheep,

and becoming quite independent of the more formal bonds with purely Indian societies. In time such people became the main element in the Spanish-founded towns, and their own small villages (plazas) and isolated farms (ranches) became the most numerous kinds of settlements in the Rio Grande Valley. Thus of the estimated 20,000 "Spanish" in 1800, only a few hundred were wholly that in ancestry as well as in faith and tongue: the *ricos* of Santa Fe and a few larger towns, officials and patrons, a few religious and perhaps a few soldiers fresh from Spain. The rest were an indigenous mixture, Mexican or New Mexican, now more numerous than descendants of either of their progenitors, and the solid nucleus of that steadily enlarging people which in later years became known as the "Spanish-Americans" or "Hispanos."

Thus geographically the over-all settled region was very little smaller in size when Spanish rule ended than when it was first imposed. It was narrowed somewhat but still as long, with formal Spanish towns and small Hispano villages and farms among the sites of the living or dead pueblos and here and there even edging out into new agricultural country, as at San Miguel del Bado, a probing on down beyond the old Pueblo frontier on the Pecos, or at Abiquiu, an outpost up the Chama to the northwest. (Fig. 2-1) Across the desert, 200 miles to the south, the El Paso settlement region was very much smaller than that upriver but now much more than a mere way-station. By the nineteenth century it was a rich riverine strip of villages and fields, the source of wine for much of the Northern Frontier and the home of several thousand mestizos and Christian Indians, the latter not only Pueblo refugees but more largely a variety of tribes and mixtures drawn from this whole plateau country. The next nearest settlement nucleus beyond was around Casas Grandes, 150 miles to the south and west, an area with close cultural ties; but commerce bound the river regions more directly south across the sand and salt deserts to Chihuahua, the main frontier market center for northern New Spain.

In 1800 these areas all seemed to be islands of civilization in the midst of vast tides of savagery which pounded upon every shore: Apaches on the south and west, Utes on the north, Comanches on the north and east. It is clear that these nomadic Indians were a much more dangerous foe in the last years of Spanish rule than in the first, for they were now in some cases mounted on horses and armed with guns, were now attracted by a much richer booty in the ranches and towns, and were everywhere deeply embittered by a long history of harsh punitive Spanish retaliations. All these Indians were certainly altered by such contacts, but none quite so advantageously as the Navaho. At first unrecorded by the Spanish, then noticed only as one of the many Apache bands hovering on the fringe of the river region, the Navaho, through increasingly extensive and close contacts with the Pueblo peoples (contacts growing out of the Spanish impact), underwent a remarkable cultural development. By 1800 they were probably more numerous than ever, adept at new crafts, and had become horsemen and sheepmen ranging over the plateau from the Jemez to the Hopi country. They had absorbed many Pueblo refugees and lived in close relationships with the Western Pueblos, but they were now recognized as a distinct people and they were troublesome raiders of Indian as well as Spanish villages along the Rio Grande.

Other Apache bands showed little interest in becoming shepherds and an ever greater dependence upon raiding as a means of living. The broad mountainous and deeply dissected plateau country between the Rio Grande and the Gila became their greatest stronghold. As such it reinforced the physical separation of the two avenues of Spanish advance into this Southwest. For during these same centuries the Spanish had also pushed northward along the Pacific slope in a movement which was superficially parallel to but rather different in character from that on the interior plateau: a gradual contiguous expansion of missions and ranches rather than a sudden leap forward to capture a remote region of Indian towns. Sonora proved fruitful ground for this process and by the late 1600's the Jesuit missionaries were working among the Pima (or Papago) Indians, thinly scattered bands of desert gatherers and marginal cultivators, along the southernmost sources of the Gila and in the deserts to the west. Eventually a presidio, missions, and ranches were established along the Santa Cruz as far north as Tucson. But the Spanish were never able to carry out such work in this Pimeria Alta to its logical limits to the main Gila Valley, with its larger body of Indians and attractive lands. By the early 1800's the vigor of this expansion was long past and only a thin population of mestizos and Christian Indians along this narrow strip exhibited the Spanish presence, a precarious foothold in the shadow of a greatly magnified Apache danger.

Thus these two Spanish thrusts deep into this Indian country did not simply establish two regions, each with a combination of the two peoples; the Indians themselves were already many different peoples and the Spanish actions increased the number and rearranged the parts to form an even more complex mosaic of Pueblo, Pima, Apache, Navaho, Ute, Comanche, and many local mixtures, Spanish and mestizo, Christian and non-Christian, an over-all design created during two centuries of turmoil and far from stabilized.

3 CONNECTIONS AND BOUNDARIES:

1820's-1860's

In the half-century following the end of Spanish rule in 1821 this broad region underwent some radical shifts in its over-all geographic situation which would greatly affect that mosaic of peoples. It was suddenly changed from the northernmost province of New Spain to the southwestern province of a new transcontinental nation, and, less abruptly, from lying as two vaguely defined and separated frontiers to two precisely defined and contiguous political areas. It was also transformed from a terminus to a pathway; from having only tenuous longitudinal ties with the outer world to a position astride several latitudinal strands within a national network. (Fig. 3-1) Viewed against a span of three centuries, what had once been a forlorn gateway to imaginary cities of gold on the barren plains became a well-trampled corridor to some very real cities of gold on the Pacific shore—for California became the new Cibola, and New Mexico and Arizona were again caught up in the quest.

COMMERCE AND CONQUEST

The shift in allegiance from Spain to Mexico caused hardly a ripple in Santa Fe, so remote from the centers of power, but a commercial corollary of that political change had an almost immediate impact which ramified through the whole region. Such abruptness was somewhat accidental. In the summer of 1821, a Mexican patrol ranging to the east encountered an American party ranging west seeking trade with

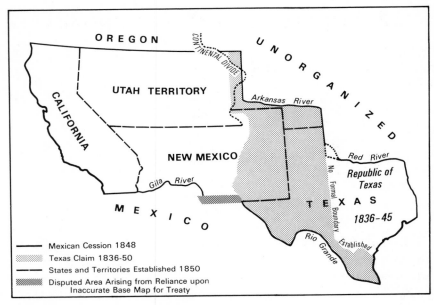

FIG. 3-1. The Initial American Framework

the Indians on the High Plains. When the soldiers explained that those doors which Spain has so rigidly guarded had just been opened by a Mexico eager for foreign commerce, the Missourians agreed to bring their goods on to New Mexico. Thus began regular contact between the Anglo-American and Hispano-American frontiers by way of the famous Santa Fe Trail.

The "Santa Fe Trail" refers to a general pattern of routes rather than a single road, for there were many possible variations across such open country devoid of settlements. Basically it was a link between the bend of the lower Missouri (at present Kansas City) and the upper Rio Grande by way of the middle course of the Arkansas. For some years Taos and San Miguel del Bado were the main portals to New Mexico. The first was a long-established center for annual fairs of the Indians of the region, and it was the nearest point for the trappers and traders who roamed the Rockies and the Plains to the north and east (as it had been for a few occasional French traders some decades earlier). The second became the principal customs station for the growing number of wagon trains which could cut more directly across the Cimarron country, skirt the high mountains, and pull over the low Pecos divide to Santa Fe.

In 1828 a trio of veteran plainsmen began Bent's Fort on the Arkansas and it became a major American outpost and an important way station. A formidable adobe structure built by Taos laborers, it was a fitting visible symbol of this cultural borderland and it was also an integral part of a rapidly developing system in support of these seasonal caravans. For the immediate success of this new commercial link was a measure of the eagerness of the New Mexicans to break the monopoly of Chihuahua merchants. Soon the Americans had resident agents and merchants in Taos and Santa Fe, and in time the Mexicans began to take their own caravans east to Missouri, where they eventually had a consul in St. Louis.

As the product of New Mexico alone was not enough to sustain much growth, American traders began to venture south. By the 1840's what had begun as a rivalry between St. Louis and Chihuahua City for the trade of Santa Fe had been so enlarged and extended as to become a rivalry between eastern America and central Mexico for the trade of the whole of northern Mexico, with American merchants and goods reaching overland as far south as Zacatecas. Insofar as European goods were involved, it became a rivalry between New York or New Orleans and Vera Cruz as ports of entry for this remote interior of North America. Thus New Mexico itself became not just a distant terminus but, for the first time, a link in a wider network. Despite the interpenetration of these two commercial systems, the balance was strongly in favor of the Anglo-Americans and their aggressive commercial tactics were a portentous display of the general power of their expansionist tendencies.

By the 1830's the tentacles of this continental trading system had been extended clear to California. A party of New Mexicans opened the pathway (the misnamed "Old Spanish Trail"), a long looping extension from the familiar routes into the Ute country beyond Abiquiu, skirting the formidable canyonlands of the Colorado then working southwesterly through the mountains and across the broad deserts to Cajon Pass and San Bernadino. A profitable trade of New Mexican woolens for Californian mules and horses, which were then driven all the way to Missouri, became a more or less annual affair for twenty years. Although never more than a minor tributary to the larger system, this lateral link was the first sustained direct contact between these two remote and widely separated provinces of northern Mexico.

In the early 1840's, Texans made several attempts to tap the trunk line of the trade across the High Plains and divert at least some of it to their ports on the Gulf. But the New Mexicans regarded these Texan expeditions as military invasions rather than commercial invitations and they killed, imprisoned, or expelled all of the members of such parties. Their suspicion of the Texans as imperialists was well founded and such episodes would prove but the opening phase in recurrent Texan pressures.

The war between the United States and Mexico grew much more out of the chronic quarrel over Texas rather than any compelling problem over New Mexico, but once under way the strategy of conquest followed directly along the paths of commerce opened a generation before. In the spring of 1846 an American army marched along the Santa Fe Trail to Bent's Fort, where it halted—poised on the Anglo-Hispano borderland—while American residents and emissaries worked within New Mexico to convince local officials of the futility of resistance and the personal advantages of withdrawal or surrender. After some weeks the army marched unopposed into Santa Fe and soon westward to help sweep the whole of northernmost Mexico into the Anglo-American nation. Most of the Mexican officials had fled to Chihuahua and a minor flare-up in Taos in 1847 caused the only bloodshed associated directly with the conquest of New Mexico.

BOUNDARIES

As neither Spain nor Mexico had ever established definite boundaries around New Mexico or California, the political definition of these areas awaited American decision. In 1850 the territories of New Mexico, Utah, and California were established, a threefold division to fit the three disparate settlement areas of the upper Rio Grande, the Wasatch Oasis (wherein the Mormons had entered in 1847), and the coastal valleys of California. (Fig. 3-2)

However, even before that gross framework was created, a severe problem had arisen over the eastern border of New Mexico. The issue was rooted in the grandiose designs of the Republic of Texas, which more than a dozen years before had claimed the full length of the Rio Grande as its western boundary, a territorial definition which would have split the settled area of New Mexico in two and put more than half of its people under the Lone Star Flag. Such pretensions were never

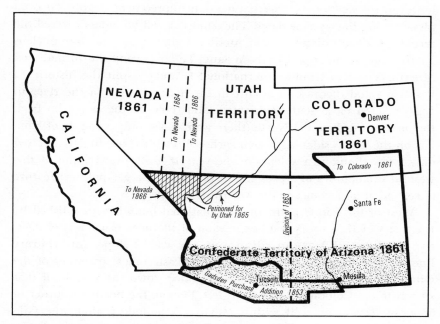

FIG. 3-2. Changes in Political Geography, 1853-1866

recognized by Mexico and were ignored or, when necessary, firmly re-
sisted by New Mexicans, and the Texas Republic never marshaled sufficient power to impose control. But immediately upon the American
annexation of New Mexico, the State of Texas reasserted this claim and
demonstrated the seriousness of its intent by sending officials from Austin to organize counties and judicial districts in all of New Mexico east
of the Rio Grande. However, that it was now a domestic issue somewhat
reduced its import, and local resistance, Congressional pressures, and
the Texan need for money resulted in a compromise in 1850 by which
Texas accepted its present western boundary in return for a federal in-
demnity of ten million dollars.

That right-angled Texas-New Mexico boundary—drawn along a
meridian (103°W) and a parallel (32°N) like many others of its era—
was the product of a Congressional committee which had little knowl-
edge of the country involved. One obvious merit of the decision at the
time was the fact that such geometry was for the most part traced
through a barren country utterly devoid of civilized settlement for a
hundred miles or more on every side. Where it touched the Rio Grande,

however, the new boundaries imposed an unprecedented political complexity upon the riverine oases. The 32nd Parallel boundary severed the recent Mexican colony in the Mesilla Valley from the old nucleus nearby and bound it politically to Santa Fe far beyond the Jornado del Muerto. The Rio Grande international boundary split the historic El Paso oasis and (because of a shift in the main channel of the river in 1837) severed most of the cultivated land (now on the east side) from the main town, Paso del Norte (there were as yet only a couple of hamlets on the Texas side). Although such political divides directly affected only a few thousand residents in the year 1848-50, the creation of this western promontory of Texas would prove to be a geo-political feature of very great importance in the American Southwest.

West of the Rio Grande, the international boundary established by the treaty of 1848 was a good expression of the northern limits of effective Spanish and Mexican advance up the Pacific slope. An arbitrary line was drawn west so as to intersect the easternmost tributary of the Gila, and thence the boundary was extended down the middle of that stream to the Colorado River. This left Tucson, the northern outlier of Sonoran settlement, well within Mexico. A boundary along the Gila divided a potentially rich irrigation district but one which was at the time so far beyond the reach of either nation that the river was selected as a convenient compromise between the more extreme initial claims of the two parties; it provided a seemingly simple method of marking a line through a country which had never been effectively controlled from any side.

The treaty-makers' reliance upon inaccurate maps, however, confounded the task of the boundary commission and reopened the dispute, and this plus sudden new developments in California led to a renegotiation of the entire problem. For even before the surveyors could begin, thousands of Americans were streaming across the northern margins of Mexico bound for the Sierran goldfields. Thus at the very outset of American rule, a latitudinal thoroughfare was suddenly imposed across the historic longitudinal lineaments of the Southwest. Therefore, instead of reflecting little more than the need for some convenient mark across a broad wasteland, the new boundary of 1853 was specifically designed to ensure American control of key features along a well-trampled pathway. In order to include the whole of the Mesilla Valley, the boundary was begun just above Paso del Norte; one hundred miles to the west it was jogged south so as to include Guadalupe Pass and several roads threading the ranges to the San Pedro and Santa Cruz Valleys; just beyond the headwaters of the Santa Cruz, at the insistence of Mexico, it was angled so as to preserve a land connection between Sonora and Baja California. Although the Americans thereby failed to obtain a frontage on the Gulf of California, they did achieve their main goal of a broad belt of territory along the southern transcontinental route.

The addition of this Gadsden Purchase quite altered the geopolitical character of the Territory of New Mexico. For the southward shift of the international boundary captured the old Hispano-Indian settlements along the Santa Cruz Valley. That northern salient of the Sonoran frontier was a realm quite apart from that along the Rio Grande. Although that historic physical separation was now modified by the new pathways to California, the current influx of settlers along that corridor from Mesilla to Tucson added a new dimension to the identification of two distinct regions. For most of these migrants were Texans, their principal interests were in cattle and the traffic to California and they were utterly antagonistic to any expression of power emanating from Hispanic Santa Fe.

Thus agitation for a separate territorial unit began almost immediately upon ratification of the annexation treaty. In 1854 a petition from Tucson called upon Congress to create a new unit—"Pimeria," "Gadsonia," or "Arizona"—out of southern New Mexico, and similar efforts were generated from there and from Mesilla during the next few years. There was always some Congressional support for such pleas, and the results of a Tucson convention in 1860 which set forth an areal and political form for an Arizona Territory seemed to be a strong indication of a likely geopolitical design for the Southwest. That plan bisected New Mexico along latitude 33°40′N and alloted all south to the new unit. That simple arbitrary boundary was actually reasonably concordant with some important geographic features. It cut across the Rio Grande Valley at the northen terminus of the Jornado del Muerto, just below the southernmost settlement in the Rio Abajo. To the west it traced through a rugged unexplored country just below the high plateaulands of the Navaho and Western Pueblos, approximating an important physical divide and placing all but the most northerly tributaries of the Gila system in the new territory; still further west it crossed empty desert. Thus to the degree that it was physically distinct, culturally disparate, and commercially dependent upon the California

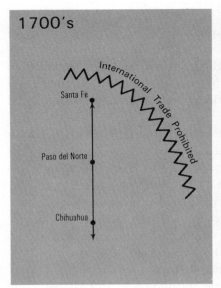

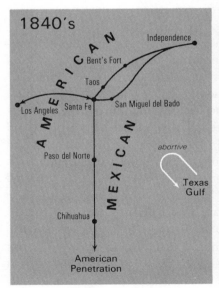

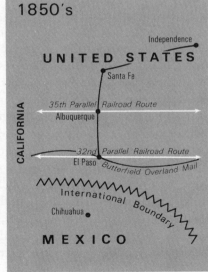

Fig. 3-3. Connections

traffic, this proposed Arizona of 1860 was by no means a grotesque design.

But this indigenous creation seemed too much a Southern corridor serving Southern interests to be approved by a deeply divided Congress.

Foundered in national politics on the eve of the Civil War, it was suddenly revived upon the outbreak. In 1861 a Mesilla convention, backed by Texas cavalry, defined anew a Territory of Arizona (slightly enlarged, with a northern boundary along 34°N), and in due course it was formally attached to the Confederate States of America (Fig. 3-3). During the next few months and especially when a Confederate army from Texas occupied Albuquerque and Santa Fe, any or all of a number of geopolitical designs, varied in source and power, seemed possible: a reassertion of Texan imperialism, a Confederate corridor to California, an Anglo conquest of Chihuahua and Sonora, an American port on the Gulf of California. But by the summer of 1862 Confederate forces had withdrawn in the face of superior Union armies from California and Colorado and a quite different framework had already received partial approval in Washington. In deference to Santa Fe interests, the huge Territory of New Mexico was now divided in two longitudinally along the 109°W meridian, a direct contradiction of the abortive Arizona design.

Although this bisection confirmed New Mexican control downriver to the tip of Texas, it had already lost an important area upstream—it had gained the Mesilla Valley but lost the San Luis. For when the Territory of Colorado was formed in 1861, Congress, with its strong predilections for symmetry, created a simple block bounded by meridians and parallels. By shifting the northern boundary of New Mexico east of the continental divide from 38°N, to 37°N, the latter became an uninterrupted political line from Missouri to California. But this arbitrary bit of tidying cut across areas of Hispano settlement and landed interests on either side of the Sangre de Cristo Range and removed from New Mexico jurisdiction over the headwaters of its natural lifeline. Santa Fe strongly protested at the time and repeatedly petitioned for the return of at least the Conejos country, that extension of the Rio Arriba district created by its own people expanding north from Taos—but to no avail.

One final boundary adjustment in 1866 affected another cultural borderland. For nearly twenty years Mormon colonists had been spreading southward into the valleys and patches of arable ground along and within the Wasatch Plateau. In the early 1860's the Church gave special support to the establishment of colonies in the subtropical valley of the Virgin River. A steamboat landing was planned at Callville near the mouth of that stream, and in 1865 the Utah legislature petitioned Congress that it be given that part of Arizona north of the Colorado River.

Arizona of course protested, but neither aberrant Utah nor empty Arizona had much influence and both lost out to expanding mining interests in Nevada for in 1866 Congress shifted the Nevada-Utah border eastward (for the third time) and extended that line south to the Colorado River to nip off the sharp-angled northwest promontory of Arizona. This seemingly minor adjustment in a distant desolate land created the "Arizona Strip" in its present form—utterly isolated north of the Grand Canyon of the Colorado—and divided the small Virgin River Basin among three jurisdictions, thereby assuring recurrent complications between Mormon settlers and Nevada and Arizona authorities.

With these alterations the gross political framework of the American Southwest was completed. The two main units were in general pattern, if not by simple intent, a formalization of the physical and historical separation of the Rio Grande and Gila basins. The Territory of New Mexico was an obvious American continuity with the Mexican, Spanish, and Pueblo past: new boundaries around an old settlement nucleus. There was little such precedence for the Territory of Arizona: Tucson was an historic outlier of Sonora; the Gila Valley was a potential rather than an actual focus, and the whole unit, with its many Indians, few Hispanos, and very few Americans, was a huge block of diverse and difficult country which had as yet no coherence. It was obvious that the new international boundary was a precise political line drawn across a broad cultural borderland and would thereby be a source of some tension and special problems. Similar discordances, apparent or incipient, between political lines and culture areas along the eastern and northern boundaries of the region would also prove to be significant. On the west, several hundred miles of empty desert separated Arizona settlements from those of California. Yet in the early years of American control it was their location with reference to California which had had the most important geographic effects upon these new territories. Within a year of their formal annexation the rush to California had begun. In the 1850's a pair of Pacific railroad routes—one west from El Paso, the other in the latitude of Albuquerque—were surveyed across the region, and within a few years each was made into a wagon road; in 1858 the Butterfield Overland Mail began scheduled service along the southern routes, and in 1866 the Atlantic & Pacific Railroad was incorporated with a view to building along the northern route. By such sinews—designed to tie California to the East—was the newly acquired Southwest being bound into the body of the nation.

4 THE CHANGING

GEOGRAPHY OF PEOPLES: 1820's-1870's

While the basic geopolitical framework was being recurrently redefined in distant Washington, the social geography was being continuously altered by a variety of local movements. Indians, Hispanos, and Anglos were all involved, each in a characteristic pattern. The major general changes were the reduction and confinement of the nomadic Indians to a few reserved remnants of tribal lands; the vigorous spread of the Hispanos broadly beyond the mountain walls of Rio Arriba and the narrow valley of Rio Abajo, a movement which was well under way before the American annexation; and the encroachment of different Anglo groups upon several sides and their strong penetration into certain sectors (Fig. 4-1). By the late 1870's the first two of these movements were essentially over and thereby, despite the continuation and magnification of the third, some of the most basic patterns of the regional social geography had become essentially set.

HISPANO EXPANSION: THE MEXICAN PERIOD

The gradual contiguous spread of Hispano colonists during the nineteenth century is a little-known event of major importance. Overshadowed in the public mind and regional history by Indian wars, cattle kingdoms, and mining rushes, this spontaneous unspectacular folk movement impressed an indelible cultural stamp upon the life and landscape of a broad portion of this Southwest. It began in a small way in late Spanish times, gathered general momentum during the Mexican

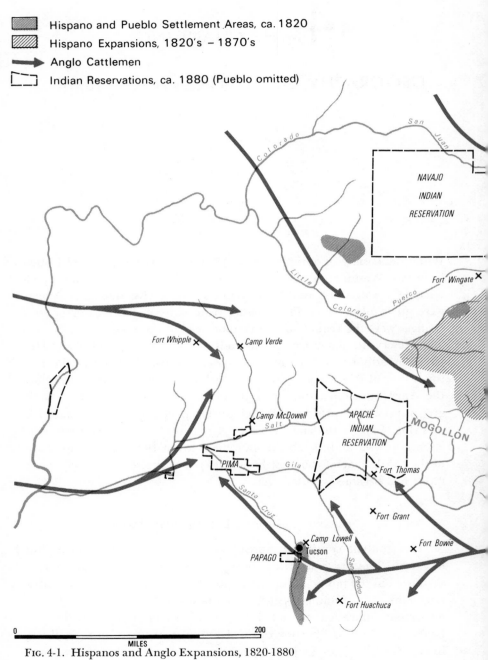

Fig. 4-1. Hispanos and Anglo Expansions, 1820-1880

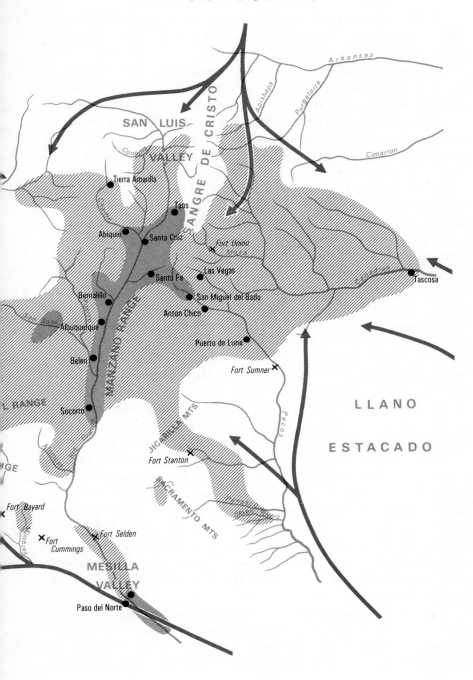

period, and continued for another generation, interrupted but never really stemmed until it ran head on into other settler movements seeking the same grass, water, and soil.

The broad canyon of the uppermost Pecos, readily accessible by an easy pass from nearby Santa Fe, proved an attractive corridor for expansion. Infiltration of Hispano settlers began in the 1790's and soon spread on past the old battered outpost of Pecos Pueblo. In a decade or two there were several hundred families in a dozen tiny placitas strung along the patchwork of terraces beneath the narrowing canyon walls. Despite occasional severe attacks from Plains Indians, this expansion continued on beyond such sheltered areas to the vicinity of Anton Chico, where it halted for a while, establishing a tentative foothold in the shallow cutlands at the head of the plains.

A branch of this southeasterly movement turned across the low southern buttresses of the Sangre de Cristo and on east and north into the folds of the foothills. In time it encountered another movement which had spread from Taos and vicinity across the ranges into the upper valley of the Mora. By the end of Mexican rule little Hispano ranches and villages—crude clusters of adobe and stone houses in a labyrinth of pole and brush corrals—were to be found in every irrigable valley for seventy miles along this eastern flank of the high mountains. San Miguel del Bado, with its large formal plazas, presidio, and customs house—expressive of its strategic location where the main Santa Fe Trail crossed the Pecos—was the local capital of the southerly section of this new eastern district. Taos administered that portion north of Las Vegas, a political division approximating the patterns of expansion.

These colonists made use of lands far beyond this sprinkle of little settlements. In the spring and early summer while the farmers turned the creeks upon their tiny fields, the shepherds drove their flocks out onto the broad plains, a seemingly endless undulating surface of tawny grass streaked by dark tongues of cedar along the crease of the ridges and the cut of the streams. It was a country at once dangerous and attractive, and this whole transmontane colonization was both a long thin shield for the Rio Arriba behind and a bold advance base for probing the great llanos beyond.

This new eastern district was the most important addition of the Mexican era but there were numerous others. There was a gradual extension of the Rio Arriba settlements north from Taos. From the Rio Abajo there was a movement east into the lee of the Manzano Mountains, placing a string of new Hispano villages in the country of the Piro Pueblos which the Indians had abandoned more than a century before. Expansions west from the river lagged behind. The country was less attractive, with broad expanses of sand and lava. Some of the better localities had long been occupied by the Pueblo Indians as at Acoma, Laguna, and Zia. To the southwest lay the most dangerous Apache country; to the northwest were the Navahos who were competing shepherds as well as intermittent enemies. Hispano herders did range out along the Jemez and the Chama, but colonists hung close to the shelter of the old settlements. Thus, although the Mexican government granted great blocks of land about as lavishly to the west of the Rio Grande as to the east, the actual pattern of colonization remained imbalanced on the side of the latter.

In 1843 a Hispano grantee received a long riverine allotment forty miles north of Paso del Norte and he soon had more than a hundred families settled around Dona Ana. Although long plagued by Apache raids, it was the first enduring colonization in the Mesilla Valley, an important nucleus in what would soon become a critical political and cultural borderland.

Despite the chronic hazards from the nomadic Indians on every front, the vigor of this Hispano expansion was a major expression of much better relations among the peoples within the older regions. The Mexican Revolution was a strongly anti-clerical mestizo uprising which put an end to relentless missionary pressures upon unwilling Indians and softened Indian-Spanish relations in general. Drawn together for mutual protection and with similar interests in colonization, all except the really hard core of the Pueblos became merged into a common population. By the late 1840's there were probably 70,000 of these Hispanos in New Mexico and no more than 10,000—perhaps as few as 6000—Pueblo Indians. Together these peoples were an island in a sea of several tens of thousands of nomadic Indians, an island connected to civilization only by long dangerous journeys along a few well-charted routes across the open wilderness. Despite the recent colonizations, these nomadic Indians were still a powerful curb upon expansion in New Mexico, and they had completely intimidated similar efforts in Arizona. Although a few large land grants had been made and several ranches begun in the upper Santa Cruz and San Pedro basins, there were too few settlers to hold the ground. By the 1840's the Apaches had driven off nearly all the cattle and most of the people, leaving no more than

a thousand Hispanos and Christian Indians huddled in the vicinity of
Tubac, Tucson, and San Xavier.

Hispano Expansion: The American Period

The conversion of this Far North of Mexico into the American
Southwest had no immediate distorting effect upon this general colonization movement. The Anglos came in as soldiers and traders but not as
yet as ranchers and farmers, and while they were quickly conniving for
legal control of the often vaguely defined Mexican land grants, they
had little prospect of developing any they might get except by means
of Hispano settlers.

The Mesilla Valley was something of an exception to this generalization, an anomaly related to its peculiar position with respect to new
political boundaries and to the infancy of the Hispano colonization.
Texans came into the area immediately after 1846. It was to escape their
pressures that many of the Dona Ana settlers moved across the river to
found Mesilla and in time a number of other villages along the west
bank of the Rio Grande (the capricious river would later shift its main
channel and put some of them on the east bank), believing, in the uncer-
tainties of the boundary situation, that they were secure in Chihuahua.
Similarly, a number of families in the oasis below El Paso crossed the
river to resettle on the Mexican side. Unfortunately for those in the
Mesilla Valley, the Gadsden Purchase made them again captives of the
United States. From time to time during the next thirty years, unrest
(arising chiefly, though not entirely, from Anglo-Hispano quarrels)
caused groups of Hispanos to seek refuge in Mexico. Indeed, except for
Ciudad Juarez (called Paso del Norte until 1888) all of the principal
Mexican settlements along the border in this area were founded by
Hispanos fleeing American soil.

But elsewhere in the Southwest there was as yet little such pressure,
the presence of American troops gave promise of greater security, and
thus in the 1850's the Hispano colonists extended their conquests rather
more boldly: north into the San Luis Valley; east a bit farther down
the upper waters of the Canadian and the Pecos; southeast past the
ruins of Gran Quivira, skirting the sand and lava wastelands into the
valleys of the Jicarilla ranges; southwest from San Marcial, at the tip
of Rio Abajo, to the Rio Alamosa; northwest through the ranges beyond
Abiquiu to the Tierra Amarilla.

The drastic reduction in Army frontier garrisons during the American Civil War had an ambivalent effect. On the west it left the Hispano settlements dangerously exposed to the Navahos and Apaches and inhibited any further advance. On the east the relations betwen Hispanos and Comanches, never one of relentless conflict, improved and in some degree flourished in the weakening of American restraints upon Indian raids eastward along the margins of settlement from Kansas to Texas. The 1860's was the great era of the "Comanchero trade," a system spanning the broad emptiness of the Llano Estacado, and one by which Comanche Indians plundered the Texas frontier, drove their stolen cattle and horses to the sheltered canyons under the rim of the Caprock, and there exchanged them for guns, trinkets, and supplies brought out by traders from such Hispano frontier towns as Puerto de Luna, Anton Chico, and Las Vegas. The livestock would then be driven to New Mexico and often on to the Colorado mines or to California. To the Texans this was a bloody criminal commerce, and a conniving with savages which could only deepen their hatred and contempt for the New Mexican Hispano. To the latter it was a continuance of fragile but long-standing trade relations with neighboring Indians—a relationship essential to peace on their own frontier—and a measure of their view of Texas as a foreign country full of potential enemies.

This controversial trade rapidly dwindled after the war. Frontier garrisons soon curbed the raiding, and then the buffalo hunters and troops together moved out upon the High Plains; in a few years the once-proud Comanches had been reduced to a broken remnant and removed to a reservation in Indian Territory. This clearing of the Southern Plains of the native herds and aggressive Indians opened the way for a surge of Hispano colonists, fanning out from their piedmont villages northeast to the Purgatoire and east across the whole breadth of the upper Canadian country, imprinting the empty plains with a thin sprinkling of their placitas, little family clusters—e.g., Garcias, Gallegos, Bueyros, Tramperos—hovering in the shallow arroyos barely below the sweep of the winds. By the middle 1870's they were as far east as Tascosa in the Texas Panhandle.

To the south, such settlers were moving in upon the main Pecos Valley. Their spread directly downriver was blocked by the Fort Sumner military and (later) Indian reservation (first established in 1862), but from their highland settlements in the Jicarilla and Ruidoso they spread sporadically down the Hondo, the Penasco, and clear to the

Seven Rivers country. Others, some from the Rio Abajo, some from the Mesilla Valley, settled in the Tularosa district along the west flank of the Sacramento mountains.

In 1863, in order to protect New Mexican settlements and keep the routes to California open, the U.S. Army began to move strongly against Indian raiders west of the Rio Grande. A methodical destruction of their flocks, fields, and orchards forced most of the Navahos to surrender and prompted their removal to a reservation at Fort Sumner. Although soon allowed to return to portions of their homeland, they no longer constituted a chronic threat to their neighbors. So, too, the Apaches were gradually pressured farther and farther back into the higher mountains. Thus in the late 1860's Hispano colonists for the first time could move west from the Rio Abajo with some security, and they lost little time in doing so. From Socorro and its vicinity they crossed the ranges, scattered along the margins of the San Augustin plains and on west into the valleys of the Mogollon, touching the uppermost waters of the Gila system. Similarly in 1871 a small group from Mesilla took root along the Rio Mimbres. Further north colonists from Albuquerque and Bernalillo soon occupied every irrigable patch along the Rio Puerco, and others ranged on beyond the Pueblo lands of Laguna and Acoma to the upper San Jose, on past Zuñi, and into Arizona. Out of the Rio Arriba settlements colonists moved from the Chama northwest across the divide into the San Juan country, and directly north to the Conejos and other locations along either side of the broadening San Luis Valley.

This vigorous centrifugal movement from the historic settlement core along the upper Rio Grande was generally halted in the 1870's. It was not a case of reaching the limits of suitable land, but of running head on into other expansions of similar character: Anglo cattlemen and Mormon farmers seeking the same kinds of pastures or irrigable ground. The initial encounters between Hispano shepherds and Anglo cattlemen were at times abrupt and severe. The relations between sheepmen and cattlemen, rarely good anywhere in the nation at the time, were particularly bad along the eastern front, where they were exacerbated by old New Mexican-Texan national and cultural hatreds. The Hispano hold upon much of their newly acquired country was necessarily thin, discontinuous, and at times no more than seasonal. The vanguard of their herders was often repelled and confined to the poorer lands, the outermost of their settlements were often soon enclaved within Anglo cattle country. The actual stabilization of the patterns of the two peoples was a long and complicated process which resulted neither in simple areal boundaries nor simple contrasts in activities (increasingly, Hispano shepherds tended Anglo-owned flocks), but it was a process which relentlessly strengthened the dominance of the one over the other.

THE INFLOW OF ANGLO CATTLEMEN

This counterforce of Anglo cattlemen moved in upon the ranges of New Mexico from Texas and Colorado. From the former they first came up the Pecos Valley, then, after the Llano Estacado was cleared and secured, broadly encroached into the upper Canadian River basin; from Colorado they moved south along the eastern base of the Rockies, then, in the wake of mining rushes, crossed the mountains into the San Luis Valley and San Juan country.

After the Civil War, the cattle drives from Texas to California were resumed, and as the army gradually brought greater security along the southern routes, there was a restocking of the ranges of southernmost Arizona and an expansion into new districts. In contrast with New Mexico, the tiny Hispano villages along the Santa Cruz never had a chance to expand into surrounding areas before Texans and other Anglos were driving their herds into all the succession of broad basins between the Rio Grande and the Santa Cruz. They then expanded northwest to the middle Gila and Salt River valleys, but here they, too, encountered competitors, as they met California stockmen coming eastward up along the mesquite thickets of the lower Gila. Severe droughts in California in the early 1870's strongly reinforced this invasion and brought in Anglo sheepmen as well. In northern Arizona there were similar movements, but with some differences in timing and origins. Some cattle from Colorado and Texas were driven in and held on the ranges along Beale's Road. But California and Utah became more important sources. Stockmen from the former came to dominate the western plateau and mountains, those from Utah controlled the high pastures around the Mormon irrigation colonies in the Little Colorado country.

Thus the ultimate effect of these several movements by Anglo cattlemen in the 1860's and '70's was an almost complete encirclement of the Hispano domain of New Mexico and at least a thin occupation of the best ranges of Arizona.

THE INDIAN REMAINDER

These vigorous expansions of the Hispano and the Anglo were at the expense of the Indian. Although the shepherd and the cowboy were usually moving in upon seemingly empty country, they were perforce occupying the hunting and gathering grounds without which the nomadic Indians could not exist. By the late 1870's only the least desirable country—barren plateaulands, rugged mountains, inhospitable deserts—remained for such people. Nor, except for a few Apache bands, as yet undefeated, were the Indians really free even within such remnant areas, for the American government was by now firmly committed to its policy of "reservations": dependent peoples held within fixed territorial enclaves under government tutelage.

Although the specific dimensions of some of the reservations would be changed, the general regional pattern was well established by 1880: the Navaho on the high dry plateau back from the Northern Corridor to California; the Apache in the heavily dissected tangle of mountains below that high rimland, and also in a portion of the isolated Sacramento ranges; the Pima and Papago in several small blocks along the streams in the lower desert country (they would later be allotted a much larger chunk of desert); and, on the western and northern fringes of this Southwest, the Colorado River Indians in several reserves from Yuma to the Grand Canyon, and the Southern Ute in the San Juan country. There was no similar vestige immediately along the eastern border, for the remnant of the once-powerful Comanche had been removed along with the Kiowa and some Apaches to a small reserve east of the Llano Estacado in Indian Territory.

These separate fragments of a once comprehensive pattern were for the most part the direct product of a brief, harsh, and often bloody series of encounters between Anglos and Indians. All the while there persisted in the very heart of the region the long-stabilized fragments of a similar encounter of centuries before. For the Pueblo Indians along the Rio Grande lived compactly upon lands formally delimited and legally confirmed successively by Spain, Mexico, and the United States. Thus, despite minor intrusions and quarrels, they were not critically affected by either the vigorous expansion of the Hispano or the powerful invasions of the Anglo. However, their more isolated kin in the western pueblos—at Zuñi and the Hopi villages—having never been brought under effective control by the Spanish or Mexicans, did experience, along with neighboring Indians, some of the afflictions brought by the Anglos before receiving legal recognition of at least the main portions of their traditional lands.

SUMMARY

Thus some radical changes were wrought in the human geography of the Southwest during this half-century, a drastic rearrangement of most of the older peoples and the catalytic introduction of some new ones.

For the nomadic Indians it was a disastrous time, ending in their defeat and capture, the loss of most of their lands and much of their freedom. Severely reduced in number and confined in area, their economies were so crippled as to make them actual as well as legal dependents of their conquerors, and their societies so weakened as to make them unable to resist some of the calculated cultural changes sought by Anglo officials and missionaries.

For the Hispanos it was a period of great demographic and geographic gains but of irrevocable political and cultural losses. Vigorously expanding, clearly the dominant people of their own broadening region, they were not formally confronted and subdued by a stronger power, but first captured incidentally as pawns in a larger game and then gradually hedged along every front by other folk movements. Although their situation was therefore far better than that of the Indians, it was nevertheless ominous since their legal hold upon their lands was precarious and their cultural status in the region had been debased.

In the 1870's the Anglos were as yet relatively few in number and were spread either very thinly or very sporadically over the region, but their power to determine the human lineaments of this region was already unmistakable. They had defined the gross political framework and overtly displayed their might in a network of military forts; they were the dominant minority in the larger towns and the aggressive majority in the turbulent mining camps and expanding ranching country. Clearly the patterns and the degree of their dominance would be determined much more by the resources they might discern than by the other peoples with whom they must share this multi-cultural region. The railroads (at that time approaching the Southwest) would provide the geographic framework for the next phase of this Anglo impress.

5 THE EARLY RAILROAD ERA:

1879-1900

The first railroad arrived at the threshold of the Southwest in 1879 and within five years the region was crossed by two transcontinental lines. Such a thrust and pattern were certainly in keeping with the national obsession for Pacific railroads which had been growing ever since the great federal surveys of the 1850's. Yet the two actual railroad companies which most directly focused their strategies upon the Southwest were not, at first, in that common pattern at all. (Fig. 5-1) Their very corporate names displayed their discordance, for the symbolic words were *Rio Grande* and *Santa Fe*, not *Pacific*; it was a difference which seemed almost anachronistic, more in keeping with the visions of the 1830's than with those of the 1870's, as if New Mexico still outshone California as a symbol of romance and riches.

The Denver & Rio Grande Railroad was born at a time when Denver interests were full of fear and frustration at having been bypassed by the Union Pacific, but it expressed the very positive geographical visions of its promoter, William Palmer, who saw his adopted city as the natural seat of an enormous tributary area forever protected from Eastern encroachment by the broad expanse of the Great American Desert. His railroad was projected from Denver to Mexico City by way of Santa Fe and El Paso, the "Mountain Base" line, as he liked to call it—a concept fitted to the continental cordillera, a longitudinal axis of empire more akin to former Spanish than current American orientations.

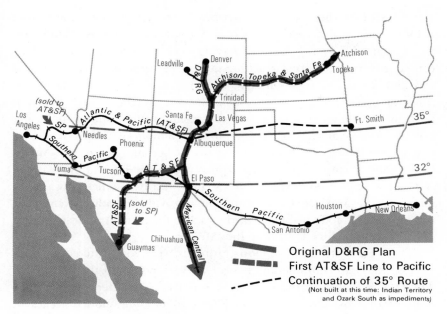

FIG. 5-1. Early Railroad Strategies

The Atchison, Topeka and Santa Fe Railroad was even more directly a modern version of an older pattern. It was originally chartered as a local project to connect the two Kansas cities of its name, but once aimed along that southwesterly route it was almost inevitable that visions would be enlarged and promoters would be lured by what seemed the inexorable logic of history to lay tracks along the famous wagon route across the plains. The company chose to follow the earlier "mountain" route up the Arkansas and across Raton Pass in order to tap the coalfields of the Rocky Mountain foothills, rather than take the more direct and easier corridor of the "Cimarron cut-off." Service to New Mexico was effectively opened when the rails reached Las Vegas on January 1, 1879. The A.T. & S.F. certainly intended to build on to or through the ancient capital, but the local terrain was such that the surveyors laid out the main line more directly westward to the Rio Grande along Galisteo Creek rather than bend it sharply northward around the flank of the Sangre de Cristo along the final stretch of the old trail. Ultimately the famous city was reached by its namesake railroad only over an eighteen-mile branch. The main line was rapidly pushed forward to the Pacific, but not in the common pattern, for it terminated at a Mexican rather than an American port, angling southward from Albuquerque and across a corner of Arizona to Guaymas. While this was in part simply the result of having been momentarily blocked by competitive interests from reaching more directly west to California, it was also a strategy representative of some important attitudes of the time: of the seemingly great commercial advantages of such Mexican ports in offering much shorter transcontinental routes; and of the rather cavalier American view of Chihuahua and Sonora as simply part of a Greater Southwest which should and would become part of the American economic empire. Similarly expressive of this latter view was the A.T. & S.F. branch down the Mesilla Valley to El Paso, where it was soon joined to the Mexican Central and thus provided another avenue for penetration—a modern version of the earlier thrust of American traders down the Chihuahua Trail deep into Mexico.

These early strategies of both railroads were soon altered, in part because they ran into one another at the very portal to the Southwest. The D. & R.G. lost in the race for Raton Pass and, after a rather fractious rivalry, by agreement turned west to tap the sudden riches of Leadville. It traded New Mexico for Colorado and by soon establishing a remarkable system penetrating and spanning the full breadth of the Southern Rockies, it transformed the Mountain Base line into the most famous mountain railroad of the continent. It did reach the Rio Grande in the river's upper reaches in the San Luis Valley and eventually sent a minor, spindly, narrow-gauge branch down through the Rio Arriba country to Santa Fe. Meanwhile the A.T. & S.F. had also changed its character. In 1880 it gained control of the Southwestern segment of the old Atlantic & Pacific project for a railroad along the 35th Parallel Route and by 1884 it had laid rails along the general line of Beale's Road from the Rio Grande near Albuquerque to the Colorado River at Needles. The Southern Pacific, which yet monopolized railroading in California, blocked its entry into the Golden State until a deal was made whereby the A.T. & S.F. traded the Arizona-Sonora segment of its Guaymas line in return for an S.P. line across the Mohave and the right to build on into Los Angeles and San Diego.

Simultaneously with these westward thrusts of the A.T. & S.F., the Southern Pacific had hurriedly built eastward from Los Angeles along the 32nd Parallel Route through Tucson and El Paso to join affiliates and connections and form a southern transcontinental line to Galveston and New Orleans.

Thus by 1885 railroads had been laid upon all the most famous of the old trails: along the old caravan track to Santa Fe, the southern roads to California, and the old Chihuahua Trail all the way from Santa Fe to Mexico City. The way was suddenly open for this Southwest to become firmly emeshed within the new commercial network of the continent.

IMPACT

The radical efficiency of the railroad could not but have a powerful economic effect upon what had been a remote and land-bound region. The most immediate impacts were upon the competitive commercial positions of the various towns, old and new, and upon mining and lumbering, where the large bulk and low value of the primary products had severely limited exploitation with more primitive facilities. Agriculture was less immediately responsive because it was as yet more in need of larger local systems for the transport of water than of a national system for the transport of its produce. Ranching was probably least affected as an industry, although the competitive market position of the wool-growers was certainly improved. Finally, while the Southwest had been visited by numerous travelers and health-seekers in the decades just before, it was the speed, comfort, and safety of the railroad car which so enlarged the volume to make such people significant contributors to the regional economy.

By 1900 mining in the Southwest was predominantly a large-scale mechanized industry controlled by Eastern capitalists and firmly established as the principal—in the large districts almost the sole—buttress of the economy. Creator of towns and industries in remote mountain and desert wastelands, its impact had ramified through the whole pattern of human geography in the Southwest. It was an industry which had evolved rapidly out of very meager, if colorful, antecedents. Aside from the small copper workings at Santa Rita and a few brief flurries of excitement over placer gold (as in the Ortiz Mountains south of Santa Fe in the 1820's), mining is a product of the American era. And here, as in so much of the West, it was a direct offspring of the great California Rush, initiated by prospectors ranging out from the Sierras and by Pacific-bound travelers diverted from the overland trails. Despite its remote and primitive state and the really formidable dangers from the Apaches the region was remarkably well reconnoitered within a decade or two, and a very large number of surficial deposits were reported. Although only the very richest and simplest of these could be worked prior to the railroads, even such gleanings supported, at least briefly, some very considerable operations, for example, the gold placers along the Colorado above Yuma in the 1850's, and those in the creek gravels of the high country around Prescott and the nuggets and ores in the desert near Wickenburg in the 1860's; the silver mines of Silver City, Clifton, and Tombstone in the 1870's; and even a few especially rich copper deposits, as at Ajo briefly in the 1850's despite the reliance on mule trains to send coke in and the crudely smelted product out across the desert and then by ships across the seas to Wales.

With such a prelude, the arrival of the railroad was followed by immediate expansion in many places and soon after, by a shift in emphasis from the precious metals to large copper deposits, a shift reflecting new industrial processes and demands as well as the new efficiencies of transport. By 1900, out of the scores of diggings and promotions, five major copper districts had emerged: Jerome, Globe, Bisbee, Clifton-Morenci, and Santa Rita, each a sprawling mass of towns and camps of several thousand people amid a complex of mines, mills, and smelters.

The arid Southwest had fewer riches above the ground than beneath it, but in a few favored places lumbering boomed as strongly as mining with the arrival of the railroad and was the basis of some new towns. By far the most extensive and valuable forests were those of the high southwestern rim of the Colorado Plateau, a narrowing arcuate strip of good pine reaching from the San Francisco mountains south and east for 250 miles to the headwaters of the Gila. Where the first railroad, the Atlantic & Pacific (A.T. & S.F.), cut through that forest, there arose the first lumber towns of the Southwest, of which Flagstaff was the most important. Essentially a product of the railroad and Great Lakes lumbermen, Flagstaff soon had several sawmills and a little later several logging railroads in operation and could ship ties, timbers, and boards.

While the railroad increased the potential value of arable land, it had no sudden revolutionary effect upon the regional agricultural economy as a whole. Only in those few areas beyond the limits of the historic Indian farmers and beyond the reach of the Hispano colonists, where productive land lay vacant and open to purchase, promotion, and development by Anglo capitalists and colonists, was the railroad a transforming tool. Thus, the greatest agricultural exhibit of the new age lay in the Pecos Valley in southeastern New Mexico. Long devoid of any settlement and unencumbered by land grant complications, by 1880 it had only barely been touched by the frontier of Hispano expansion and sparsely occupied by Texas cattlemen. Thus the relatively large river and its long floodplain quickly attracted the attention of developers, who laid out comprehensive programs, and within a few years there came into being an entirely new agricultural district with an extensive irrigation system, railroad branch, and thriving towns and farms. By 1900 there were 8,000 people in the valley, and once the orchards matured and the facilities for sugar beets and other crops had been fully developed, expectations of the agricultural export were very great.

Less sudden but somewhat larger and even more promising was the development of the Salt River Valley in central Arizona. Here, too, Anglos were the pioneers, moving in in the 1860's upon lands just north of the Pima farmers along the middle Gila. That they were only reoccupying the lands of an ancient agricultural people was evident in the settlement ruins and the clear tracings of old canals along the valley (these needed only to be re-excavated a bit to be put to use in some places), and in recognition of this fact they named their first town Phoenix as a fitting symbol of life rising anew from the debris of the past. But there could be little growth based only on the local mining and military trade before the railroad arrived in 1887. The first modest boom soon followed, accompanied by a considerable expansion of acreage and the first experiments with citrus crops, Pima cotton, and winter vegetables, alhough alfalfa remained the principal crop. By 1900 there were about 20,000 settlers in the valley, a quarter of these in Phoenix, the rest on the farms and in the several small towns recently platted.

There was really nothing comparable to the Pecos and Salt River Valleys elsewhere in the Southwest. In most of the rest of New Mexico, although Anglo newcomers got legal title to more and more of the land, most of the readily irrigable portions remained densely occupied by Hispano farmers who were conservative, fearful, and bitterly resentful of relentless Anglo encroachments, and who persisted in their old ways as far as possible. The commercialization of northern New Mexican agriculture would obviously be a slow and uneven process. Only in the Mesilla Valley, where the Hispano colonization had only just begun before the Anglos first arrived, was there room for any considerable Anglo colonization. There the entry of the railroad enhanced the value of the land, stimulated commercial farming, and so heightened the pressures upon the Hispanos that sixty families left Dona Ana in the 1880's to resettle in Mexico. But many more stayed on, and this first important Anglo agricultural foothold along the New Mexican Rio Grande remained a home for both peoples thereafter.

Another group of agricultural invaders, already famous as the first Anglo-Americans to establish a society based upon irrigation, arrived in the Southwest about the time of the early railroads, but the expansion of the two was completely unrelated. The Mormons were in some ways more like the Hispanos than like other Anglo settlers: small tightly cohesive clusters of subsistence farmers who had searched out a few marginally habitable spots amid the Southwestern wastelands and lived isolated and alienated from the encompassing national society. Mormon penetration of this Southwest began in 1875 and quickly spread into several districts. The first footholds were in the upper hills of the Little Colorado wedged between the Navaho and Apache lands, but there was so little irrigable land that within a few years small groups of families had spread on east into half a dozen localities widely scattered from the San Juan to the Mogollon. The more important expansion was southward down through the rugged country below the Colorado rimlands to the upper Gila. As only a few Hispano and Anglo settlers had taken root in this area, as yet so recently in the very midst of Apache country, the Mormons found several miles of good riverine lands available and were soon well settled and supplying local mining districts with produce. Another stream of migration came out of Utah to the Salt River Valley in 1877 and obtained a foothold just east of the small town of Phoenix; in the following year, a small dissatisfied party from this colony ranged on farther southeastward and settled in the San Pedro Valley at St. David. In the 1880's some families from all of these colonies as well as some prominent members of the Utah hierarchy established a series of colonies across the border in northwestern Chihuahua and northeastern Sonora as refuges for those fleeing federal authorities bent on suppressing polygamy.

Those Mormon colonists constituted an important new element in the social geography of the Southwest but by 1900 had as yet had relatively little impact upon the regional agricultural economy. Both the nature of their society and the character of most of the places they settled put severe limitations upon commercial development.

The railroads brought the last big influx of cattle into Arizona, both to the north and the south along the main routes. By far the most spectacular example of this movement was that of the Aztec Land & Cattle

Company, a syndicate of A.T. & S.F. officials, Eastern bankers, and Texas cattlemen, which purchased a million acres of the Atlantic & Pacific land grant in northern Arizona and shipped in about 40,000 head of cattle from Pecos, Texas, to Holbrook. As Navaho, Hispano, and Mormon settlers and stockmen were already scattered over that area, and as the land grant purchase gave the cattle company legal title only to alternate sections rather than a single large block of land, there were immense complications, and the sudden arrival of the "Hashknife Outfit" (as the company was known, from its brand) was bitterly resented as a "Texas invasion." But this was the last big importation, for by the late 1880's all the ranges of the Southwest were heavily overstocked, and the dry years and depression of the early 1890's led to sharp reductions and the gradual transformation into a more stable ranching industry, with fenced pastures, irrigated haylands, and improved breeds.

Regional Structure, c. 1900

By 1900 the Southwest was emerging as a more coherent functional region. It was bound together by a simple grid of railroads in which the two latitudinal transcontinentals were linked by two local longitudinal lines, one in New Mexico and one in Arizona. (Fig. 5-2) Only two relatively minor peripheral areas lay outside the reach of that network and its branches: the Pecos Valley and the San Juan, each a corner of New Mexico tributary to other circulatory systems. Furthermore, the fact that this Southwest system was set apart from others by broad expanses of nearly empty country to the east and west emphasized its separate provincial character. Only in the northeast where lines focused upon Denver reached south into Hispano country was this Southwest regional system directly challenged by another.

The chief trade centers of the region were all located on that main grid, though not necessarily at its four main junctions. In the east they were at those strategic points, at Albuquerque and El Paso, each at an historic crossroads of the river valley axis with a transcontinental route; but in the west they were not, for there was no comparable physical or historical channel and the lateral rail line, when finally completed in 1895, wound its way over and around a tangle of mountain ranges to forge a new link between north and south in Arizona. Access to a productive hinterland as well as location on a trunk line railroad was necessary for commercial eminence, and thus here Prescott and Phoenix

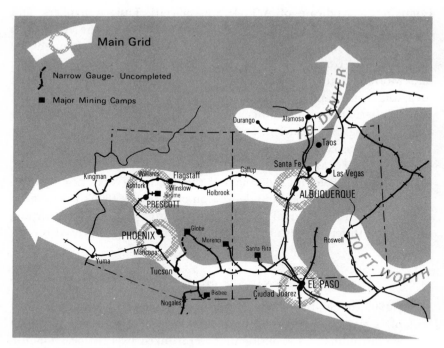

Main Grid

Narrow Gauge- Uncompleted

Major Mining Camps

TO DENVER

Durango

Alamosa

Taos

Santa Fe

Gallup

Las Vegas

Kingman

Williams

Flagstaff

Ashfork

Winslow

Holbrook

ALBUQUERQUE

Jerome

PRESCOTT

Globe

PHOENIX

Morenci

Roswell

Maricopa

Santa Rita

Yuma

Tucson

TO FT. WORTH

Bisbee

Ciudad Juarez

EL PASO

Nogales

FIG. 5-2. Regional Structure *c*. 1900

continued to be the main centers and were in no way threatened by the creation of Ash Fork and Maricopa at the rail junctions.

By strongly affecting both the patterns of access and of production, the railroad could not but affect the relative power of the various trade centers as well. In New Mexico the most marked effect was the triumph of Las Vegas and Albuquerque over Santa Fe and Taos as the principal centers of commerce, although it should be emphasized that the railroad only accelerated and completed a trend which had been developing for forty years. By 1900 the results were plain to see. Taos failing to get even so much as a branch line, had faded into a purely local center. A few Anglo artists and tourists had come to appreciate this picturesque cluster of Indian pueblo and Hispano villages as a colorful and historic place, a kind of living museum of a fascinating cultural past, but it was so well away from the main pathways that its quiet life was as yet little disturbed.

Santa Fe did not have to be rediscovered for it never lost its fame as the historic Spanish capital, but the entry of the railroads doomed its commercial pre-eminence and that, in turn, even threatened its political position. For as soon as the A.T. & S.F. was completed, Las Vegas commanded all east of the Sangre de Cristo, and Albuquerque all to the south and west. Furthermore, the latter town with obvious logic saw itself as the new crossroads of the territory and its rapid economic growth prompted it to aspire to become the political center as well. Through the application of adroit maneuvers and ample money within the labyrinth of territorial politics, Santa Fe was able to defeat the attempt to shift the capital, but even more protracted and lavish efforts failed to bring it the commercial position it coveted. It took large public subsidies to induce the A.T. & S.F. and the D. & R.G. to build their branch lines into the town, but attracting the former only averted the disaster of being entirely bypassed, and the latter proved to be a tortuous narrow-gauge, long delayed in completion and of little value once in operation. All of Santa Fe's efforts to bind New Mexico economically once more to itself were thwarted by a ring of competitors now better situated within the railroad network: Alamosa, Las Vegas, Albuquerque. What had for so long been an advantageously sheltered and pivotal position within the Rio Arriba had quickly become a relatively inaccessible and eccentric one within the new traffic patterns of a greater Southwest; and even though it continued to be the focus of the most densely settled Pueblo and Hispano districts, that now meant only that it was also the center of the most conservative and backward economic area in the whole region.

Long before any railroad had even gotten started in the direction of Santa Fe, Anglo merchants had become well established around the plazas of all the important communities in the region. Sustained at first principally by Army contracts and payrolls and the needs of California emigrants, they later prospered from the Indian Bureau and other federal agencies, gradually captured the expanding wool trade, and in general became the complete commercial intermediaries between the industrial world and these provincial outposts. The railroad brought in new merchants and speculation and by expanding the range and scale of trade and competition led to a greater concentration of such trading companies into a few growing centers. An excellent example of such a firm which came across the plains and entered New Mexico simultaneously with the railroad as joint heralds and agents of the new economic era was that which began as Otero & Sellar, a Kansas partnership between two men who had worked together in a Leavenworth wholesale house, the one a New Mexican of Spanish parentage, the other a Midwestern Scots immigrant. Setting up in business at the end-of-track on the Kansas Pacific near Ellsworth in 1867, they moved their outfit year by year as the railroad crossed the plains, and in 1873 shifted south to the new A.T. & S.F. line which had then reached Grenada, Colorado, and thence followed its progress to La Junta, El Moro, and, finally, in 1879, to Las Vegas, where they decided to set up permanent shop. Two years later the firm was sold to its local Anglo manager and became Gross, Blackwell & Co., which for the next twenty years, through a network of branches and affiliates as far afield as Clayton and Magdalena, competed for trade and engaged in land investment, resource development, and local finance over nearly the whole breadth of New Mexico. In 1900 it was but the largest of many similar mercantile and trading companies which dominated the local economy of the Southwest.

Las Vegas (population *c.* 6000 in 1900) and Albuquerque (6238) became by far the greatest centers of such commercial houses. To some extent they competed for the same territory, but for the most part each served a large local hinterland, Las Vegas reaching south and east as well as commanding the Sangre de Cristo foothills country, Albuquerque reaching down the valley and far to the west. Together the two hemmed in Santa Fe, and the railroad line from the north did more to drain the Rio Arriba country to Colorado than to confirm its focus upon the ancient capital.

Las Vegas and Albuquerque were not only similar in strategic position and commercial function, they were alike in plan, scene, and society. In each case the railroad passed a mile or so east of the original settlement and the result was two towns, Old and New, sharing the name but sheltering different societies, vividly distinct in age and architecture: the unkempt cluster of flat-roofed adobe huts and shops along the narrow pathways radiating from the old Hispano plaza now suddenly paired with the formal blocks of Victorian façades lining the graded streets and sidewalks leading to the new depot. (Fig. 5-3) Physically the towns soon grew together along the main street, linked by horsecars and a busy traffic and looking more alike as the new architecture encroached upon the old plaza, but they persisted as two parts of a whole, Hispano and Anglo, separate social communities bound into an economic entity.

In contrast with these dual towns, Santa Fe (5603), while obviously much affected by the Anglo intrusion, remained a single city. Here old

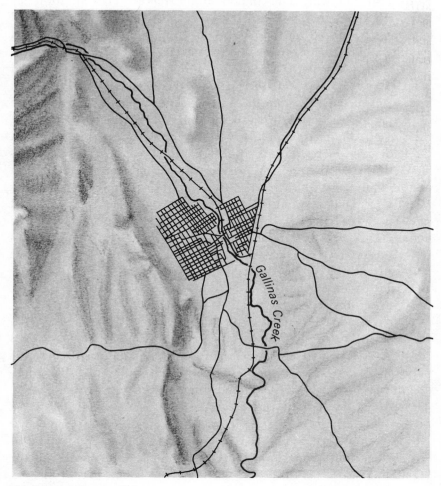

Fig. 5-3. Las Vegas, 1893

and new were closely intermingled with ornate stone business blocks adjacent to old low adobes, and American Greek Revival federal buildings opposite the utterly plain piles or baroque façades of early Hispanic institutions. These and many other patterns were a physical expression of the more intimate intermingling on more socially even terms of Anglo and Hispano in the business of governing the territory they shared.

Old town and New, Hispano and Anglo, were apparent at Paso del

Norte also, but with some important differences. The old town lay across the Rio Grande but it had a new name—Ciudad Juarez—as well as many new people and businesses, reflecting the new era of political stability and economic growth and the new importance of international traffic in the Mexico of Diaz. El Paso, on the American side, was an old name given to an essentially new city, for there had been no more than a set of hamlets here before the railroad, but its population was more Hispano than Anglo. Its 16,000 people made it rather more than twice the size of Albuquerque or Las Vegas. It drew some sustenance from the local oasis, more from its strategic position as a military and commercial focus on the international border, but most of all from a rich mining hinterland which reached from central Arizona to central New Mexico, bringing ores and concentrates, coal and coke, to its mills and smelters and serving as an expanding market for the big mercantile houses. One special feature of El Paso was the fact that although it was fully Southwestern in character, it stood on Texas soil and thus was politically divorced from the region it served, a geographical discordance which was of major importance to the political balance of power within New Mexico.

Tucson, oldest of the cities of Arizona and still the largest (7531) was repeatedly frustrated in attempts to enlarge its tributary area. Its eccentric location and strong identification with a Southern Democratic political faction caused it to lose the territorial capital and, like Albuquerque, to be given the territorial university as a small consolation. The marked decline of Army activity in the region after 1880 was a further political factor affecting its trade. Although it was prominently astride the southern trunk line, it was unable to bring even southeastern Arizona into strong focus. For the railroad system turned all the big mining districts of the area, even Bisbee and Globe, toward El Paso, which was closer to coal for smelting and to the East for all kinds of supplies and markets. Even the Mexican trade through Nogales was turned to Benson and the east more than down the Santa Cruz valley to Tucson. The most ambitious project to capture a much larger share of the mining trade, the Arizona Narrow-Gauge, designed to reach north to Globe, was a scandalous and costly failure. Thus while Tucson was by no means completely shut out of serving such districts, it was sustained by a much smaller area and trade than its historic and natural position might seem to warrant.

Phoenix, the second largest city (5544), was in the midst of the largest cluster of population in the territory. Being relatively central within the political area was certainly very important to its successful effort to secure the capital, but being central within the largest irrigable area was more fundamental to its economic and political future. By 1900 there were half a dozen smaller communities in the Salt River Valley and there was clearly a potential for much further development of this tropical oasis.

Over the mountains to the north, Prescott (3559), older than Phoenix, once the largest Anglo center, and twice the territorial capital, was prosperous but dampened in its larger aspirations. It lost the capital in 1889, six years before it got a railroad connection to central and southern Arizona, while it still lay cramped in its mountain setting relatively inaccessible to the main areas of population growth. The completion of that railroad lessened that isolation but could do little to enlarge very greatly its commercial prospects. With Phoenix to the south and the string of trunk line towns to the north, Prescott was left dependent upon local mining, lumbering, and ranching districts, a relatively rich but rather narrowly restricted tributary area.

A series of towns had sprung up at fairly regular intervals along the track of the old Atlantic & Pacific, the California trunk line of the A.T. & S.F. between the Rio Grande and the Colorado. Although identical in age and in many ways similar in appearance and function, each locality also had its differences: Gallup with its coal mines and Indian trade; Holbrook, the big ranch supply center; Winslow, the railroad town; Williams with its sawmills; Kingman with its desert mining trade. Flagstaff (1271) was the only one which in some degree transcended its local area. Although it was the largest of the lumber towns, its outreach to a wider region was probably more due to the accidents of history than to any special advantages of geography. Among those accidents, the arrival of the five Babbitt Brothers from Cincinnati in the 1880's was probably as decisive as any. They made Flagstaff the headquarters for what was soon the largest mercantile firm in the area, with branches in all the larger towns from Holbrook to Kingman, trading posts in the Indian country, and a network of operations that included dealings in livestock, wool, meat packing, lumber, and hotel-keeping as well as the distribution of Eastern goods. Typical of the mercantile capitalism of its time and region, such a firm was an agent and symbol of Flagstaff as the main focus for an extensive though thinly populated realm.

These several small cities were the principal commercial centers of the Southwest, each pre-eminent within a considerable area and in various degrees competing along border zones. Despite rather large differences in size (for example, between El Paso and Flagstaff) there was little to indicate that any one or two were emerging as the dominant center or centers for the whole Southwest. New or old, large or small, none were more than provincial outposts of Denver, Kansas City, Houston, or Los Angeles and San Francisco.

6 REGIONAL

SOCIAL GEOGRAPHY, c. 1900

By the turn of the century people had spread over all the habitable Southwest and were busy exploiting and developing all the resources in their power. But aside from a few major mineral districts it was not a bountiful region, and it had undergone nothing like the influx of population and booming growth characteristic of so many other parts of the West. A population of 350,000 in 1900 was only slightly more than double that of 1880, a comparatively modest total and growth for the first twenty years of the railroad era. Nevertheless, that total included a greater variety of peoples than any comparable area of the West, and that growth had significantly altered some proportions between older and newer groups; thus a new social geography continued to emerge concomitant with this developing economic geography (Fig. 6-1).

VARIETY OF PEOPLES

The several small cities which had developed were not only local points within a national network of commerce, they were inevitably local centers for the Americanization of regional cultures. Whether New Towns only in part or in entirety, they were the chief exhibits of the Anglo presence, the points of injection and the centers for diffusion of the people, objects, and ideas of an aggressive national culture which was exerting pressure upon every people of the region, no matter how ancient, and penetrating every corner, no matter how remote.

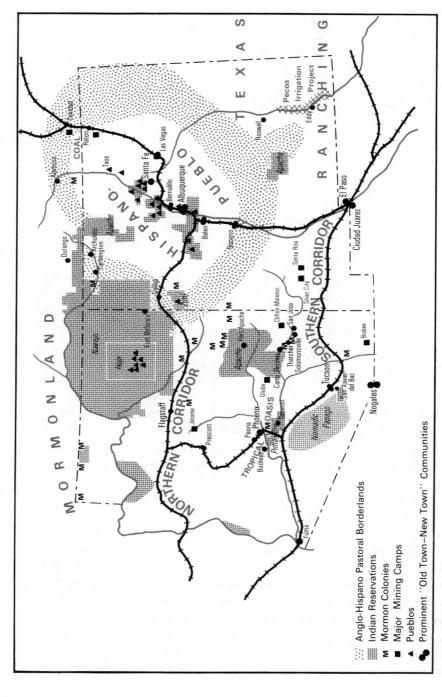

FIG. 6-1. Social Geography c. 1900

···· Anglo-Hispano Pastoral Borderlands
▓▓ Indian Reservations
M Mormon Colonies
■ Major Mining Camps
▲ Pueblos
● Prominent "Old Town–New Town" Communities

By 1900 the generality of three peoples—Indian, Hispano, Anglo— was in detail a mosaic of very nearly a dozen. The Indians were still in four main groups: Pueblo, Pima-Papago, Navaho, and Apache, each mainly in particular reserved areas, and each with special characteristics and problems. Yet at this point they exhibited so many common results of the heavy impact of the Anglo conquest that it is appropriate to speak in general about them. The turn of the century was, in fact, near the nadir for Indian life in the Southwest. The demographic deformations and social disintegrations of several decades of warfare and relocation, disease, alcohol, and starvation were starkly apparent. Their reserved lands proved far from inviolable. Stockmen encroached almost at will across every border, railroads were given permission to build across reservations, and whole chunks of land had been taken away by abrupt decree, as in the contraction of the San Carlos Apache Reservation to release the mineral lands on either side around Clifton and Globe. Formal contacts with Anglos were focused at the agency towns, such as Fort Defiance, Fort Apache, and Sacaton, each with its federal officials, missionaries, schoolteachers, and traders, designed to be centers for supervising and civilizing the "savages." Even well-intentioned Anglo efforts, such as missions and boarding schools, often had strongly schismatic effect upon local tribes, while the lure of jobs on ranches and in towns began to pull increasing numbers off their old tribal grounds and out of their old tribal ways. Yet the Indians still numbered at least 40,000 and occupied, if only very sparsely, very large areas, and although each group was but a deformed remnant of its earlier society, there were sufficient numbers and sufficient evidences both of tenacity and adaptability to suggest that they would remain a major and distinct element in the social geography of the region.

The Hispanos, bound together by language, religion, and a proud social heritage, had greater cohesion as a group than either the Indians or the Anglos, yet Anglo economic development was indirectly responsible for the first important geographical and social division within the Spanish-American peoples: between the old, deeply rooted peasant agricultural and pastoral society characteristic of northern New Mexico on the one hand, and on the other, scattered clusters of Hispanos in the big mining camps, many of whose members were recent immigrants from Mexico and all of them recent migrants to these localities. The one group was stable and tenacious, a full society dominating whole counties, overtly resisting Anglo pressures and still a strong political force; the other was landless and leaderless, little more than fragments of an older society, living entirely at the mercy of the Anglo economy but almost entirely outside of the Anglo society and polity.

While to the Indians and Hispanos all the rest were Anglos, these too were in several more or less distinct groups, differing in source and society and tending to settle in different sectors of the region. The largest was composed of those of Middle Western or Eastern back-grounds, representatives of that heterogeneous mixture which was suffi-ciently blended together and was so centrally important to the national culture as to be generally acknowledged as "typically American." Com-ing most especially out of Kansas, Missouri, and Illinois, often after a sojourn in Colorado, such people brought with them, remained in touch with, and were ever quickly responsive to, all the leading styles and trends in the national culture. Those who came by way of Texas were a second group. It was a migration which drew from the entire South but was largely Texan in number and strongly Texan in type. Although obviously Anglo-American in general, whenever such people settled together and maintained their older ways, they were as obviously a special regional type, differentiated by political and racial attitudes, religion, and social mores, a society even more expansive and aggressive and less cohesive than that so typical of the nation.

Less clearly distinguishable in kind were those who came in from the West. Although most Californian Anglos had been born elsewhere—and chiefly in the Middle West—they seem to have been transmuted by their contact with the dynamic, heterogeneous, fluid society of the West Coast. Experimental, optimistic, and aggressive, they saw potentialities in the Southwestern subtropics less apparent to others and brought with them attitudes and methods which left their mark upon mining and agriculture, towns, tourism, and politics.

Still another group, Anglo in general but obviously distinct to all, were the Mormons, proud adherents of their own peculiar faith, a so-ciety so at variance in certain ways with the American norm that it was generally regarded as a national problem. There were perhaps 10,000 of them in this Southwest in 1900, but they had an influence much greater than their numbers. Industrious, literate, highly organized under capable leaders, they were so cohesive as a group and so concen-trated in a few localities that they were major elements in the economic, social, and political geography of larger districts. While other people tended to regard them as alien intruders, they saw themselves as outposts of the new Zion, and thus while other Anglos competed for power in Phoenix every Mormon had his place in a hierarchy centered in Salt Lake City.

There were a few other clusters of distinctive peoples here and there, such as the Cornish miners at Globe, or coal company towns full of Slavs and Magyars recruited and transported en masse from Pennsylvania, but these were small and localized in comparison with the others and could not be considered major pieces in the regional mosaic.

One other group, though relatively few in number and very widely scattered in location, touched the lives of all these other peoples and was fundamental to the whole development of the region: the Jewish merchants. Although "Anglo" in the broadest sense, these people also maintained an identity. Entering in the wake of the American Army, they began their tireless search for business wherever it might be found. Well before the arrival of the railroad their mercantile houses dominated the plazas of every important town (when Otero & Sellar set up shop in Las Vegas in 1879, Ilfeld, Stern, Jaffa Brothers, Rosenwald, Dold, Brunswick, and Rosenthal were already there). By 1900 they had penetrated the entire Southwest: there was "the Jewish pueblo trading post; the Jewish sutler; the Jewish storekeeper in almost every settlement; the Jewish sedentary merchant of the cities who sat at the peak of the business hierarchy; the Jewish drummer peddling his way through every village and town and as often as not to every ranchhold" (Parish, 1959, p. 326). Cosmopolitan and acute, educated and adaptable, respected if not always admired for their success, yet so few and so scattered as to escape most of the traditional ethnic animosity, such people were at once leaders and intermediaries and have been described as "catalytic agents" in the cultural as well as commercial development of the Southwest. As a distinct people in intimate and critical contact with all the others, they were in a strategic position for the promotion of cultural harmony. By helping to bind together Anglo, Hispano, and Indian, helping to adapt old ways to new, helping to link desert outposts with the industrial metropolis, these versatile persons were the principal architects in the formation of a functioning regional society from an array of disparate parts.

SUBREGIONS

The social geography of 1900 was a reflection of the different areal combinations and proportions of this diversity of peoples. It was not of course a neat pattern of discrete parts, for such subregions were never uniform in content or sharply separated in areas, yet it was a general pattern so apparent and so basic to so many public issues of the time as to be well recognized by many residents.

The largest and in many ways most important of these subregions was the Hispano-Pueblo area, still firmly rooted in the old core along the river and extending out in all directions over the Hispano pastoral lands, a compact contiguous block covering half of New Mexico. The entire perimeter was an unstable zone of varying width where Anglo and Hispano stockmen still contested for control of grazing grounds. Because the railroad was here built through a region already well colonized, it created only adjuncts to old towns rather than wholly new ones, and Hispano-Anglo contacts were very largely focused on the Old Town-New Town pairs spaced along the track. The larger of these, such as Las Vegas and Albuquerque, obviously contained two complete communities side by side, interdependent but socially segregated, the single large Catholic Church and the parochial school looming over the one, balanced by the churches of half a dozen Protestant sects and the public school in the other. In smaller towns the Anglo sector might be no more than a few shops and houses with few or no social facilities, but even when it was no more than a new depot opposite the old plaza of a small village, this dual cultural structure was visible.

Santa Fe was the sole example of any extensive intermingling of the Hispano-Anglo sectors and it was also an example of how these two were not everywhere simple synonyms for Old and New, for here the big Romanesque cathedral and cluster of Catholic schools and convent were little older than their Protestant and public counterparts and represented the initiatives of a new bishop and priests sent from the United States and Europe to breathe new life into an old Hispano ecclesiastical body which had become markedly ingrown and warped during a long period of isolation. The most notable evidence of deviant development was to be found in the back valleys where the Penitentes, a highly organized ritualistic secret brotherhood, still held a good deal of prestige and power. Sprung from earlier movements in the Church, the New Mexican Penitentes had evolved into a local folk cult which was now proscribed but far from suppressed by Church authorities. In many of the villages in the mountain country, the Penitente *morada* (chapel) still stood alongside the Catholic church.

Any of the Hispano settlements away from the railroad would likely have at most a handful of Anglo (most likely Jewish) shopkeepers and perhaps here and there a Protestant missionary working fruitlessly among those whom he considered to be near heathen. In the back valleys there were whole villages essentially untouched by the larger world, while in the pueblos, even those within sight of the passing trains such as Isleta and Santo Domingo, a hard core continued to live entirely in the old ways, thus far as successfully resistant to Anglo as they had been to Spanish intrusions.

In 1900 the Hispanos were still a very large majority in this area, yet despite gross inbalances in numbers, here the three peoples faced one another on more even terms than anywhere else in the Southwest. For it was here that both Indian and Hispano had their strongest, deepest roots and their most richly elaborated societies and thus were best prepared to sustain the shock of the Anglo cultural impact. Furthermore, here the Anglos came very largely as merchants, professionals, and officials rather than as ranchers and farmers. They came to exploit but not to expel, avidly conniving for titles to land but not needing to settle upon it themselves to the exclusion of others. Further still, they were mainly from the Midwest and East and already included some persons who had a sympathetic interest in these older societies. Although much of the efforts of such people now seem patronizing and crude, they at least represented some attempts to work with or for the Hispanos and Indians rather than against them.

The Northern Arizona Corridor was related to but separate from this large region of northern New Mexico: there was the same Anglo trafficway, but here carried beyond the realm of Indian and Hispano villages, creating across an ancient but virtually empty Indian land a string of Middle Western towns along the Kansas-born railroad. Gallup, founded by the railroad near the western reaches of the Hispano and Pueblo country and the southern margins of Navaho lands, was strongly geared to the Indian trade and stood as a link between the two regions. Beyond was an almost purely Anglo swath in which the towns, each literally astride a national thoroughfare, were relatively open, heterogeneous, and cosmopolitan. In this area the Mormons were still largely within their own tight little communities and most of these, as well as the Hispano and Texas stockmen, were located considerably south of the railroad. All along the north lay the desolate Indian lands, partly formalized into reserves for Navaho, Hopi, and Hualpai, and everywhere bordered by the awesome terrain of the canyonlands which walled off this whole side of the Southwest from all commercial contact to the north, a wilderness crossed only by an occasional Mormon party on a lonely journey to or from Utah, a feeble pulsation along the thin arteries serving the extremities of Zion.

The Southern Corridor was in some respects an obvious counterpart to that in the north: a string of railroad-created towns—Deming, Lordsburg, Wilcox—along an Anglo route across the old Apache lands. Texas ranchers had spread over the whole area, and in population and orientation it seemed a modern version of the old abortive Arizona Territory scheme binding together the Mesilla and the Santa Cruz valleys. Here, too, as in the north, there were Mormon enclaves lying back from the main line. But there were major differences also which complicated the regional pattern. Tucson, the old focus of southern Arizona, was largely Hispano in population but strongly Anglo in business and leadership; with its urban axis connecting depot and plaza and with the Pimas, Apaches, and the Christian Indians of San Xavier a persistent part of the surrounding scene, it was more a counterpart of Albuquerque than of Flagstaff. Unlike northern Arizona, in Tucson the Hispanos were a major element in the population of the region but, unlike northern New Mexico, not primarily a rural population. There were farm villages in the Mesilla Valley, the Santa Cruz, and in a few scattered places, and there were a good many Hispano ranch hands, but mostly these people were here as an industrial laboring class, clustered around the mines, mills, smelters, and railroad yards.

Much of the social geography of this subregion was mirrored in miniature along a sixty-mile stretch of the upper Gila Valley, a sort of "pocket" just north of the main corridor: from Clifton and Morenci, the one cramped along the narrow canyon floor and the other clinging to the mountainside high above, old mining camps now stabilized by the big copper works, permanent towns full of a fluid conglomeration of peoples; to San Jose, a dozen miles downstream, a tiny isolated Hispano agricultural village; to Solomonsville, a relatively old Anglo town named after an early Jewish merchant, the county seat and chief trade center along the newly completed railroad branch; to a solid strip of Mormon farms and villages focused upon Thatcher, the seat of the local church leadership with its big meeting house and academy; to Camp Thomas, the Army post guarding the portal of the Indian reservation; and finally on beyond to the clusters of brush *ramadas* of the captive Apaches. Over the countryside on either side of this riverine strip, prospectors roamed the mountains and Texas ranchers held the foothills and plains. It was a rich human diversity which expressed half a dozen different movements of the past quarter-century.

The railroad trunk line west from Tucson passed through desert country, serving only a thin scattering of ranches and minor mineral districts, with no town of any importance before Yuma, the small oasis at the Colorado crossing. Just to the north, however, lay the central Arizona oasis which was rather socially distinct from districts to the south and east. The Mormon colonies at Mesa and Lehi and the Indians (Pimas) on their small reservations were not uncommon elements, but there were few Hispanos and none with any historic roots in the area. Furthermore, the influences from California appeared to be greater than those from Texas. The string of young towns from Tempe to Peoria and Buckeye with their largely Middle Western population lured to tracts and towns by shrill land promoters made the scene more akin to Los Angeles than to the older Southwest.

These several broad areas were the main pieces in the general social geography of the Southwest but there were, in addition, several fringe areas within the arbitrary geometric bounds of New Mexico or Arizona which were in character or in commerce more closely related to bordering regions. The largest of these was the Pecos Valley which was shared by Texas ranchers and Middle Western agriculturists. There were no Indians and very few Hispanos, and it was a more homogeneous Anglo-Saxon Protestant population than to be found anywhere else in the Southwest. Roswell was typical of ranch-supply centers in West Texas, while Eddy (now Carlsbad), the instant town of the irrigation company, with its full complement of churches, schools, courthouse, and a clause in every deed prohibiting the sale of liquor, was like a bit of Kansas transplanted. The fact that the rail lines led south to the Texas & Pacific or northeast to Amarillo and had no direct connection whatsoever with the rest of New Mexico strongly sustained the Texas-Midwest character of the area.

In the northeast was another corner which lay just beyond the grasp of Hispano colonists. Raton and its coal town satellites in Colfax County were entirely similar to those found along much of the Colorado piedmont. Anglos ruled the rangelands, the Hispanos having been excluded from the area partly through the effects of the huge Maxwell land grant which had come under the control of European speculators who fostered Anglo development.

The San Juan corner of New Mexico was another remarkable mosaic of peoples: Ute Indians on their reservation just north of the river,
Navahos on theirs just to the south, Mormons along the river at Fruitland, Hispanos at Blanco and Archuleta, with Anglo colonists and
traders at Farmington and Bloomfield in between. The Navahos and Hispanos were mainly sheepmen, the Anglos (from Colorado and Texas)
were cattlemen, and the Mormons were farmers. Although this combination of peoples was not untypical of the Southwest, commercially the whole district had been turned toward Colorado upon the
completion of the Alamosa-Durango railroad line, and it was thus one
of the border regions tapped by the D. & R.G. after it had been deflected
from its original New Mexican strategy.

Finally, in the most remote corner of all were the tiny Mormon footholds south of the Utah border in the high block of country north of
the Grand Canyon in Arizona, inaccessible and completely isolated from
all but their Mormon kin in the Virgin Valley.

POLITICAL UNITS

This discordance between social geography and political geography
around the borders of the Southwest was not as yet of great importance
simply because all of these areas were rather thinly settled and contained
only a tiny proportion of the total population of the territories. Much
more important politically was the old discordance between the major
social subregions and the two political units of New Mexico and Arizona, the federal territories established in 1863.

Arizona itself did not have really serious internal sectional problems. The Anglos were completely dominant and although there were
differences in background among those of the north (mostly Midwestern), center (many Californians), and south (Texans and Southerners),
they tended to work well together in order to block the two political
minorities, the Mormons and Hispanos (the Indians did not have the
vote), from exerting any influence. The fact that the Mormons were in
all three areas was a special spur to co-operation, while the fact that the
Hispanos were very largely in the Southeast somewhat undercut the
power of population numbers in those counties.

Once the Prescott-to-Phoenix railroad was completed, giving a lateral link between the two east-west axes, Phoenix was an excellent site
for the capital: central and accessible, with good prospects for further

colonization and growth in the local area. Its selection also probably helped reinforce the strong Californian influence and orientation in the territory. Although the copper and lumber industries and the A.T. & S.F. were primarily controlled by Eastern interests, the Southern Pacific was Californian and the mining laws, county government, and many political and social attitudes had been strongly influenced by California. In 1887, one-third of the members of the territorial legislature were either natives of, or had come to Arizona after residence in, California.

New Mexico, on the other hand, was chronically plagued with the tensions between north and south. It was not a simple Hispano-Anglo antagonism, for both peoples were represented in both areas, but it was an expression of the inclusion of two distinct cultural and economic areas within a single political unit. A method recurrently proposed to solve the problem was to redraw the political boundaries. In the 1870's interests in the southwestern corner of the state centered upon Silver City memorialized Congress to be annexed to Arizona, citing common concerns with mining and the Apaches, the easier access to a capital (which was then in Tucson), and their desire to live under a more "American" (i.e. Anglo) government. It was an obvious local recognition of the realities of a Southern Corridor region in contrast with Hispano-dominated northern New Mexico. So, too, was the attempt in the 1880's to create a Territory of Sierra out of the southern counties of New Mexico and the western tip of Texas, a political area which would have been firmly dominated by Southern Democrat cattlemen. This western promontory of Texas was a very important feature in the political geography of the Southwest. For had El Paso been in New Mexico, it would have given the dissident southern part of the territory a much greater focus and cohesion, and although it still through all these years would have been a minority section, it would have been sufficiently augmented in population and power as to have brought north and south into greater balance and made territorial politics necessarily much more the work of a Santa Fe-El Paso axis than merely the "Santa Fe Ring."

This internal tension was a persistent complication to the issue of statehood for New Mexico, a national and territorial question which loomed large during these years. In general, the Anglos of the southern counties opposed statehood out of fear of domination by the Hispanos of the north, whereas the latter were fearful that merger into the federal body would only accentuate their minority position within the nation and bring even heavier pressures upon their institutions. As a result, when a vote on the question of admission was taken in 1890 it was soundly defeated in both sections: by the Hispanos of the north led by the local Catholic church which saw its parochial school system threatened, and by the Democrats of the south who did not wish to be an Anglo minority under the domination of Santa Fe. The national Congress, without looking closely at these internal sectional problems, was reluctant to admit New Mexico simply because its dominant Spanish-speaking Roman Catholic population seemed "un-American." The whole statehood issue was of course enmeshed in national politics and by no means did it hinge only upon local conditions in the territories. Certainly the prospect of four new senators representing so small a population (in 1900 only 195,000 in New Mexico and 123,000 in Arizona) was an obstacle to admission. Whatever the balance of reasons at the turn of the century, these two Southwest units, together with Oklahoma and Indian Territory, were the only remaining territories amidst the otherwise solid body of 45 states.

Although it is convenient to think of a Southwest standing as a discrete part of the gross regional framework of the nation, an Anglo-Hispano-Indian realm bound together by its railroad grid and set apart by nature and people from its surroundings, there was really little conscious feeling of regional unity within. Those who lived there were far more aware of the subregional differences: the Anglos of Arizona grateful to be separate from Hispano-dominated New Mexico; while in New Mexico, Anglo and Hispano alike were obsessed with the tensions between north and south. Yet the national public was made ever more aware of the existence of a "Southwest"; for by any measure, to any resident east of the High Plains it was a strikingly unusual region. The promoters of this "Sunset Land" and "Sunshine Country" had a great problem finding adjectives sufficient to describe the spectacular scenery in contrast to the situation, as in some other areas, of finding anything sufficiently unusual or attractive to describe. Furthermore, here man as well as nature was a distinctive part of the scene. Indians of one sort or another were to be found in most areas and the Hispanic flavor was widely apparent. Inevitably, the most accessible of the most exotic subregions got the most attention. Shortly after railroad service was inaugurated, a guidebook published in Kansas City proclaimed the wonders to be seen in the Hispano-Pueblo country of New Mexico, offering complete "descriptions of towns, pueblos, churches, pictures, statues, ruins, and antiquities; together with mountains, canyons, springs, and other places of interest." Of the largest city it noted that "while the 'new town' will attract the merchant, the tourist will be drawn to Old Albuquerque," and that among the landscape features which would be most striking to the stranger were the "adobe (a-do-bay)" houses, the abundance of small donkeys or "burros (boor ro)," and the many quaint churches. While the details of this particular part could not be generalized into a very accurate depiction of the whole Southwest, they could appropriately serve to emphasize a strong areal differentiation from the rest of the nation.

7 PATTERNS OF ECONOMIC

DEVELOPMENT: 1900-1970

Few American regions surpass the Southwest in the proportionate changes wrought in the scale and pattern of its economy and demography over the first seven decades of the twentieth century. As in the nation as a whole, the regional history of that span can be rather sharply divided into two phases by the irruption of World War II, an event which was responsible for some altogether new features as well as for the strong acceleration of some older trends. In the following sections no attempt is made to measure these developments in economic terms but rather to describe those which are significantly related to further important changes in the regional social geography. (Fig. 7-1)

AGRICULTURE

Shortly after the turn of the century a sequence of wet years and an enthusiasm for some new techniques of "dry farming" gave rise to a renewed confidence in the agricultural conquest of the Great Plains and sent a new wave of settlers spreading into its farthest western fringes across the northeast boundaries of New Mexico. It was a colonization movement strongly promoted by companies which purchased large blocks of government and railroad lands and vigorously recruited settlers in the Midwest and Texas. One of the most notable areas was the Mesa, a high grassland lying just east of the upper Canadian River which had been bisected by a railroad to the Colfax County coalfields in 1902. Although Hispano sheepmen had been using the area for thirty years, they owned very little of the land and were powerless to halt this invasion of farmers. Within a few years the high plains surface had been converted into grainfields served by a string of new towns along the railroad, such as Mosquero and Roy, and it stood as a large Anglo island surrounded by the shallow cutlands along the creeks spotted with tiny Hispano villages from which the sheepmen now ranged over only the rougher, poorer pastures.

Another area of similar sudden invasion at this time was the Estancia Valley, a broad dry basin lying east of the Manzano Range. Here, too, a railroad built through the area en route to other destinations opened the country for Anglo colonization schemes. With artesian water for households and gardens and the special cultivation techniques for conserving the natural soil moisture, it was expected that these heretofore parched and empty lands could be converted into a highly productive district. And here, too, although the area was unpopulated it was not unused, for it was the seasonal grazing grounds for all the Hispano villages along the eastern flank of the Manzano Range. By 1910 these villages were paralleled by a new Anglo series along the railroad in the floor of the valley—Willard, Estancia, Moriarty, Stanley—and the former Hispano pastures had been cut up into homestead blocks and sown with grain, corn, and beans. Numerous small sprinkles from this same general wave brought Anglo settlers into a wide scattering of localities, such as along the northern flank of the Capitan Mountains in south-central New Mexico, and in the Sulphur Spring Valley of southeastern Arizona. Occasionally these settlers would clearly imprint their identity upon the maps with such names as Texas Park and Kansas Settlement. The village of Miami, along Rayado creek in the Cimarron country, was an Ohio name implanted in the old Maxwell Grant by a colony of German Dunkards in 1907. (Miami, Arizona, a much larger and very different sort of town, was laid out about this time on Miami Flats, so named by some Ohioans in the Globe Mining District.)

None of these colonizations was entirely successful. In some areas dry farming was a failure in all but unusually wet years, and in most it was marginal at best. Some of the settlers shifted more to livestock than farming, picking up land abandoned by former neighbors; in other areas only a much more extensive and expensive shift to irrigation made it possible to stay. Thus in all of these localities the sudden influx was soon followed by a straggling exodus, but in all of these former pasturelands there was left behind at least some permanent Anglo settlement in a drastically altered setting.

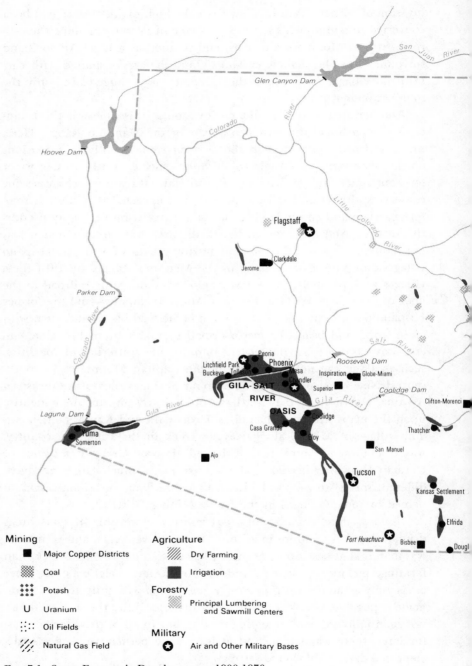

Fig. 7-1. Some Economic Developments 1900-1970

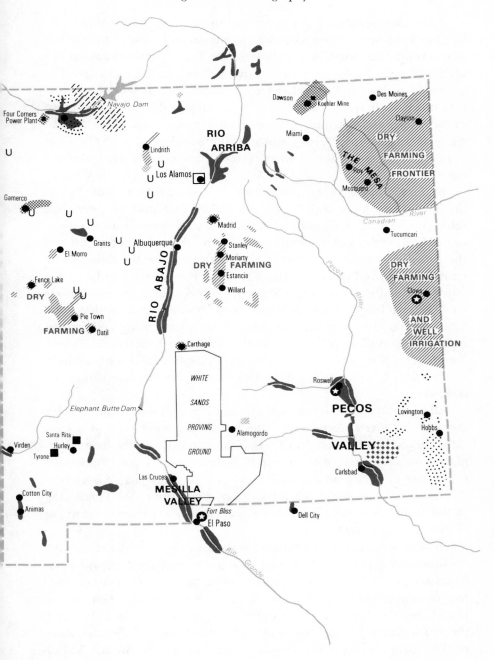

A decade or so after this first wave of dry farmers came a second, related in kind but moving more solidly and securely into a new sector. It was simply the colonization wave on the Llano Estacado rolling out of Texas as far as the western rim overlooking the Pecos Valley. The success of shallow wells on that high flatland made it possible to convert much of it from a grazing to a farming realm, replacing range cattle with grain, sorghum, peanuts, and various truck crops. A relatively dense pattern of farm towns soon dotted the area, with Clovis, at a junction of two railroad lines, quickly emerging as the principal center.

Beginning in the 1920's, and reinforced in the 1930's by those fleeing the severe droughts in their Texas and Oklahoma homelands, were still other tiny streams of migration which trickled into much more remote and difficult corners of the Southwest, such as along the eastern edge of the Jicarilla Reservation, along the southern flanks of the Zuñi Mountains, and here and there over the high bleak plateau country far to the south toward the Datil ranges. Picking up homesteads on government lands among Hispano and Indian grazing grounds, such settlers combined dry farming of grains and beans with cattle raising and formed scattered but distinct little communities such as at Lindrith, El Morro, Fence Lake, Pie Town, some of them recognizable Anglo hamlets, others marked by no more visible focus than a schoolhouse, church, or cemetery.

All of the aforementioned colonizations involved some degree of dry farming and thereby represented the frayed outermost edge of a basically Middle Western pattern of agriculture carried onto the desert margins of the Southwest. After about 1915, however, the most important expansions in agricultural colonization were in a few major irrigation districts developed under federal auspices, expansions which indicated an Anglo and national adoption of the ancient Southwestern technique of living in dry lands.

In New Mexico, the first important work of the federal government was the redevelopment and expansion of the Pecos Valley irrigation system after floods had badly damaged the earlier private networks. So, too, the construction of Elephant Butte Dam on the Rio Grande enlarged and stabilized irrigation agriculture in the Mesilla Valley and the El Paso oasis. In the Pecos such works merely assured the expansion of the Anglo developments already under way; in the Mesilla Valley the rise in land values resulted once again in strong pressures on the

Hispano farmers and led eventually to further Anglo control of the area.

Developments in Arizona had a considerably greater impact upon the economic and social geography of the region. By far the most important were the several programs undertaken over a period of twenty years to expand the reliable supply of water available for the rich desertlands of the Salt River and middle Gila River valleys. The completion of the Roosevelt Dam on the Salt River in 1911 was the major key to the early phase, as the completion of the Coolidge Dam on the Gila was to the later one. By 1940 there was an almost continuous broad arc of highly developed irrigation lands from Eloy and Coolidge on the south and east, to Peoria and Buckeye on the north and west. And not only the scale but the character of agriculture had been greatly altered. Although alfalfa remained a staple, cotton, citrus, and winter vegetables had become firmly established as major commercial crops, while dates, though less important as a source of income, were probably the most effective of all as an advertisement of Arizona as a truly tropical oasis. Similarly, the construction of the Laguna Barrage across the lower Colorado greatly expanded and stabilized the production of such crops on the floodplain and benchlands below Yuma. As with dry farming there were many much smaller colonizations based upon the harnessing by dams or wells of lesser water supplies. Most of these were private projects, sometimes undertaken by a land company which then recruited settlers, sometimes by a group of settlers themselves, as at Virden on the upper Gila, established by Mormon families forced to abandon their Mexican homes during the chaos of the revolution.

The total of these developments in the first four decades greatly enlarged the role of agriculture in a region wherein it was everywhere faced with rather severe limitations. Although every expansion of plowland meant a diminution of grazing land, the net effect upon the livestock industry was ambiguous. The dry farming of such cash crops as wheat and beans was a direct encroachment but much of the irrigated land was devoted to fodder and thus was complementary, allowing significant increases in the quality, and in some places in the numbers, of stock on adjacent rangelands. The kinds of livestock continued to reflect in some considerable degree cultural preferences: the Navahos, Hispanos, and Mormons specializing in sheep; the Anglos and the Apaches in cattle.

Contrary to the trend in most activities, agriculture has undergone

only minor changes in the years since World War II. Further abandon-
ments of marginal dry farmlands and extensive consolidation of those
farms remaining has reduced the rural population in northeastern New
Mexico. In the southeast the expansion of well irrigation has supported
considerable increases in the Llano Estacado. Less important in total,
but quite dramatic locally, has been the initiation of deep-well irrigation in a series of arid bolsons along the southern border of the region
from the Salt Basins west of the Guadalupe Mountains to the Sulphur
Springs Valley west of the Chiricahua. The conversion of such parched
rangelands into highly productive cotton fields and the appearance of a
series of new hamlets, such as Dell City, Cotton City, Animas, and El-
frida, is the result of the most recent in the sequence of preponderantly
Texan colonizations along this Southern Corridor.

On the other hand, the older and larger irrigation districts have experienced little expansion at their edges because of the lack of new
feasible sources of water, and some have experienced considerable contraction internally because of relentless urban encroachments on both
land and water. Such competition is especially acute in central and
southern Arizona, and it is a contest which under current economics
and attitudes agriculture cannot hope to win.

Mining

Roughly contemporary with the new developments in dry farming
and the new federal irrigation programs early in this century was the
development of new techniques in the recovery of copper which made
it profitable to work very low-grade ores. Such operations required a
whole new scale and complex of facilities—huge open pit mines served
by railways, new types of mills and larger smelters—which in turn required a much larger labor force and a major expansion of towns to ac-
commodate them. Such mining districts came to have a more or less
standard set of settlement components: an old town which bore the
marks of many years of fluctuation as a mining camp; a small formal
new town for the Anglo officials, engineers, and foreman; a sprawling
unplanned workers slum; and a new formally planned company-owned
smelter town. In some of the newer and smaller developments, the first
of these components was missing and the rest were grouped in a single
loose cluster, as at Ajo and Superior. In others these several parts were
separated from one another by varying distances. Because of fumes and

slag, the new smelters were usually located several miles from the mines and thus a number of new names—Clarkdale, Hayden, Inspiration, Hurley, Douglas—appeared rather suddenly on the map of the Southwest as towns of considerable size. Douglas was the oldest and largest of these, a wholly new settlement laid out by the Phelps Dodge Company adjacent to a huge new smelter poised on the international border to receive copper concentrates from both Bisbee and Nacozari. Except for Jerome, where operations have ceased, the big copper districts of 1900 still dominate regional production, but there are many others of importance, some now over half a century old (Superior, Ajo); others large but very new (San Manuel); still others once important then long idled and now reopened on a major scale (Tyrone).

Developments in mining, railroads, and the general increase in population, prompted major expansions in the Colfax County coalfields, where Dawson was but the largest of several company towns; and also in a scattering of smaller fields, such as at Gamerco, near Gallup, Carthage, east of Socorro, and Madrid, south of Santa Fe, where the rows of identical little steep-gabled wooden houses shipped in prefabricated from Kansas were a sudden discordant Anglo imprint on the old Hispano landscapes of the Cerrillos. But changes in technology and the competition of other fuels have more recently brought about a complete abandonment of many of these operations and sharp reductions in nearly all the others. Only where the most modern techniques are well adapted to a specialized purpose is coal mining still important, as in the case of the Koehler Mine in Colfax County, which produces coking coals for the Kaiser steel plant in California, and the new Four Corners plant for the production of electric power, on Navaho lands near Farmington. Furthermore, the degree of automation and the lengthy commuting range of workers have meant that even in such cases no new big coal towns have appeared in the stead of the many old ones now gone.

In contrast, the discoveries and continued expansions in production of coal's great competitors have brought about major alterations in the economic and settlement geography in two corners of New Mexico. Beginning in the late 1920's a series of rich oilfields has been opened on the edge of the Llano Estacado and in the Pecos Valley, transforming the farm hamlet of Hobbs into a booming city and the chief economic center of the industry in the state. Similarly, in the 1950's major discoveries of oil and natural gas in the opposite corner brought 20,000 people into Farmington, a small trade center in the remote San Juan

Basin. These industries are very largely Texan. In the southeast corner the railroad to Lovington, the pipeline network, the oil companies, oilfield workers, and accompanying businesses were all an integral part of the enormous dynamic Texan complex, making the oilman, like the cattleman and the farmer before him, but the latest to expand routinely westward beyond an arbitrary state boundary which had been drawn across the natural continuities of grass and soil and geological formations. By the 1930's the cumulative result was the creation of "Little Texas" as the most distinct and homogeneous subregion of New Mexico.

Two other mining productions have had important but much more localized effects: potash on Carlsbad (formerly Eddy), and uranium on Grants, which in the 1950's grew from a ranch supply town of 500 people to become the nation's largest uranium milling center with a population of 10,000.

INDUSTRY AND GOVERNMENT FACILITIES

As a relatively thinly populated region remote from the main national areas of industrial production and consumption, the Southwest has been heavily dependent economically upon the primary resources of the soil and subsoil, with the processing of its materials limited to that necessary for efficient shipment. Such is still the case in regard to the treatment of local raw materials, but there are now whole new realms of industry which are relatively free of such restraints. These industries have enjoyed a dramatic growth recently in the Southwest, and their initiation was very closely related to activities of the federal government initiated thirty years ago. The magnitude of the Indian wars and the chronic tensions between the United States and Mexico had long made military installations a prominent part of the Southwest scene and important buttresses to the local economy. However, by the 1930's their number and importance had been greatly reduced and the sudden huge reassertion in 1940's was only to a small degree bound to older patterns, such as at Fort Bliss, adjacent to El Paso, and Fort Huachuca, west of Bisbee, both old permanent border garrisons. For the new military posts were in no way a response to local problems but rather more essentially industrial establishments requiring a labor supply and service facilities. Thus the big air bases and ordinance works were chiefly near the large cities, as at Phoenix, Tucson, Roswell, and Flagstaff. With the continued national emphasis on military developments most of these installations have not only been maintained but have been expanded and thus remain prominent points of economic and demographic growth (although the air base at Roswell was closed in 1967).

However, by far the most important and radical impact was made by the facilities established for the development of the most important and radical innovation of the Second World War: the atomic bomb. These occupy three quite different types of location, each suited to a particular phase of the operations: Los Alamos, the summer camp transformed into a city to serve as the scientific headquarters, easily guarded in its mountain isolation, yet easily reached by car thirty miles northwest of Santa Fe; White Sands Proving Grounds, a large accessible wasteland which was transformed from a desert liability into Alamogordo's main source of sustenance; and Albuquerque, the general headquarters, an urban environment with all of the facilities for local services and national communications. All of these have been enlarged and continued under the Atomic Energy Commission and together with the few military installations account for more than 20 per cent of the income of the total labor force in New Mexico.

Closely related to the development of such federal activities and to the radical growth in the labor force has been the emergence of an array of wholly new industries. Electronics and aircraft are by far the most important and characteristic: using skilled labor to produce complex items of small bulk or high mobility and heavily geared to government contracts. Phoenix and Tucson are by far the most important centers of such activity but small plants can be found in every subregion, and even on the Navaho Reservation.

TOURISTS AND SOJOURNERS

Whereas the new clusters of scientific laboratories, electronics plants, and aircraft testing facilities have been basic to the phenomenal economic and demographic changes of the past generation, the motel and roadside restaurant, dude ranch and golf and country club are far more common exhibits of a growth industry now nearly a century old. For such accommodations so heavily bordering the highway today are but the current counterparts of the depot hotels and souvenir shops, rustic camps and sanatoria of the railroad age.

The tourist traffic was well developed by the railroads, but it necessarily focused upon a few points and areas either on or easily acces-

sible from the mainlines: the Pueblo-Hispano regions around Santa Fe
and Albuquerque; the Navaho and Pueblo country around Gallup; the
Grand Canyon (the railroad branch to the South Rim was completed in
1901); the Spanish and desert environment of Tucson; and the tropical
oasis of Phoenix. The A.T. & S.F. was long the most effective advertiser
of New Mexico and northern Arizona, creating a strong image of a land
of colorful Indian and Spanish peoples and natural wonders. It built a
series of comfortable hotels and maintained a variety of off-line bus
tours, such as its famous Indian Detour which gave the visitor a glimpse
of many of the pueblos and ruins in the Santa Fe-Taos area. In the
1930's the inherent flexibility of the bus and automobile began to
spread this kind of tourist traffic into every part of the region. Even the
comparatively drab and monotonous southeastern corner of New Mexico found a powerful attraction in its underground spectacular, Carlsbad Caverns, discovered in 1901 but not nationally publicized until
1925 and not developed as an accessible tourist attraction until the next
decade. By 1940 every town and hamlet on a paved road in the Southwest had its gasoline stations, roadside lunch counters, souvenir shops,
and auto courts to lure the ever-greater traffic, and the extent of the
road network, the capacity of such facilities and the volume of such
traffic has strongly increased every year since the end of World War II.

Other special qualities of the Southwest attracted people who were
rather more than tourists and who became a steadily expanding element
in the region's population and economy: those who came for longer so-
journs to partake of the presumed special curative powers and amenities
of its sunshine, air, and waters. Montezuma Hot Springs, where the
Santa Fe Railroad built a handsome hotel shortly after it had reached
nearby Las Vegas, was the first major resort to be developed for such
purposes. By 1900 those afflicted with "consumption" or other ailments
considered peculiar to the damp climates of the East were a prominent
component of both the seasonal and permanent Anglo populations in
the region, living in elaborate resorts, modest cabins, or humble "tent
cities." However, although government and philanthropic organizations
continued to maintain various facilities, the active recruitment of such
persons faded rapidly with the growing realization that tuberculosis was
a highly communicable disease. But the clear mountain air and the
warm desert sunshine continued as powerful lures of people who came
with less serious afflictions or who simply sought to escape the rigors of
weather back home. The sojourners of northern New Mexico and north-

ern Arizona came mainly in summer; those of the southern half of the region mainly in winter. Such seasonal migrations were vigorously promoted by railroads, resorts, and chambers of commerce, and the volume of traffic grew rapidly after 1920 to become a major economic support of many localities. Improved highways, air service, and the general American affluence have simply compounded such trends in recent years, while the wide use of air conditioning to cool the summer heat, and the great upsurge in the popularity of skiing in the winter snows, have in some degree modified the formerly sharp seasonality of the traffic to the two types of areas.

Thus serving those who come but do not stay continues to be a really fundamental component of the regional economy. In Arizona in the 1960's, for example, the income produced by "tourism and travel expenditure" was approximately equal to that produced by agriculture. And in fact the two were to some extent interdependent, for it was estimated that half of the cattle ranches in the southern part of the state were also in some degree dude ranches.

TRAFFICWAYS AND TRADE CENTERS

The basic regional structure of trafficways of 1900, a simple grid with the main commercial centers near the four junctions, was still easily discernible in 1970, but a few new routes, new methods of transportation, and, especially, radical differences in proportionate growth among competing trade centers had produced some important modifications. (Fig. 7-2)

The first interregional addition to the early grid was made in 1908 when the A.T. & S.F. built a line from Belen directly east to Clovis to connect with its Texas lines and then, a few years later, completed another short link within Texas to make a direct route from Albuquerque-Belen to Houston-Galveston, and thereby a California to the Gulf of Mexico trunk line competitive with that of the Southern Pacific. In the 1920's, however, the latter company reciprocated by acquiring a local line northeast from El Paso which connected with a long feeder of the Chicago, Rock Island & Pacific. Soon the S.P. and the C.R.I. & P. were jointly featuring a Chicago-to-California route directly competitive with the main line of the A.T. & S.F. Thus the trunk line patterns of each of the two great Southwest railroad systems were developed in a giant "——<" parallel to one another but some distance apart all the way

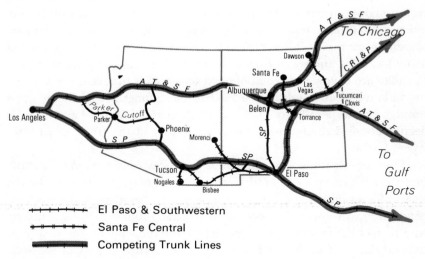

+ + + + + +	El Paso & Southwestern
+·+·+·+·+·+	Santa Fe Central
▬▬▬▬▬	Competing Trunk Lines

Fig. 7-2. Later Railroad Strategies

across half the continent, with Albuquerque-Belen and El Paso at the respective junctions binding California, the Midwest, and the Gulf together.

Another new interregional link which would only gradually grow in importance was the Parker Cut-off, which gave the A.T. & S.F. a more direct line between Phoenix and California, avoiding the tortuous route via Prescott.

Some of these and other more local constructions had important effects upon the competitive positions of certain major trade centers. Las Vegas proved the most vulnerable, for the railroads angled across the Canadian and Pecos areas from Texas severed a large part of its former trade area, and apportioned it among Tumcumcari, Santa Rosa, Clovis, and Roswell, leaving Las Vegas to stagnate within a very local hinterland. Santa Fe, hemmed in from the very start of the railroad era, made a costly attempt to reach out and tap the country to the south by means of the Santa Fe Central Railway. Projected to Roswell and El Paso, it was actually built as far as Torrance, a hundred miles, but through a country so lean—even after the colonization of the Estancia Valley—that it was a loser from the start, unable to push on farther and inconsequential in its effect upon Santa Fe's commerce.

In contrast, El Paso's commercial position was enhanced by the very extensive regional system of the El Paso & Southwestern Railway, built primarily to serve the copper operations of the Phelps Dodge Company, which reached out as far as the Dawson coalfields to the northeast and Morenci, Tucson, and Bisbee to the west. It was a system of such intrinsic value and competitive potential that it was purchased by the Southern Pacific in 1924. Tucson gained a direct line up the Santa Cruz to Nogales, but it was an international connection which would only gradually grow in importance.

Just as the railroad network was being brought into final form, another network, new in kind but largely imitative in route, was emerging. Although the maps of the early 1920's show an extensive pattern of roads with numbers and names pertaining to a network, only Albuquerque, El Paso, Tucson, and Phoenix had more than a few miles of paved all-weather radial highways. Not until the early 1930's did the main strands of a larger network actually emerge in function in this region, but thereafter highway development was so rapidly accelerated that by 1940 paved or well-gravelled roads touched every important district, and a heavy interregional and even transcontinental traffic was being carried along these latest versions of the old pathways across the Southwest. The interstate system of superhighways now being completed is in general simply the newest version of the older routes, with Interstates 40 and 10-8 paralleling Routes 66 and 80, and the A.T. & S.F. and S.P., (extending from Barstow, California, to Little Rock, Arkansas, Interstate 40 is the most complete expression yet of the 35th Parallel Route of the Pacific Railroad surveys of the 1850's). The main addition to these latitudinal avenues has been the great rise in the importance of the Phoenix-Los Angeles connection, now the western segment of Interstate 10, following the older Route 60-70 and, in effect, the equivalent of the still earlier Parker Cut-off of the A.T. & S.F. (Fig. 7-3)

The lateral linkage in New Mexico remains the same, the new Interstate paralleling the Rio Grande as did its predecessors, but in Arizona, Interstate 17 is significantly new for it provides a direct link between Phoenix and Flagstaff, by-passing Prescott. Thus Flagstaff's position, now at the very junction of the main grid, has been in some ways enhanced at the expense of Prescott which, like Las Vegas, New Mexico, has had to give up its regional commercial aspirations.

The southerly extensions of these lateral lines, the oldest routes of all but long minor in importance, have shown a strong increase in traffic. The enormous number of border crossings recorded at El Paso-Juarez and Nogales of course largely reflect the local daily movements within these bi-national metropolitan clusters, but the interregional commercial

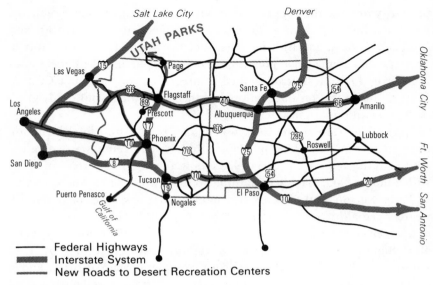

FIG. 7-3. Highways

and tourist traffic has also greatly increased in recent years, probably chiefly the result of greatly improved facilities in northern Mexico.

Among the newer additions to the over-all network, still very much secondary in importance yet very indicative of other new patterns affecting the region are a trio of lengthy routes fanning out of Phoenix to distant resort and recreation centers: north to Lake Powell and the Utah parks, northwest to Lake Mead and Las Vegas, Nevada, and southwest to Puerto Penasco on the Gulf of California in Sonora. Each is a trafficway across the broad belt of wastelands which so long served as a rather formidable regional boundary, and each is an illustration of how deserts and canyons and arid coasts are being converted from barriers into attractions and thus new points of interregional contact.

While the general persistence of the basic grid of circulation has served to stabilize trade areas, the gross differences in internal growth of the main trade centers have brought some changes. The major development in the commercial geography of the past twenty-five years has been the phenomenal development of Phoenix. Its volume of wholesale as well as retail business is now more than double that of any other city in the region, and although this business is derived largely from central Arizona, the great increase in efficiency of highway transportation with the completion of the interstate system will certainly allow a strong penetration of northern Arizona to the detriment of Flagstaff, and the sheer size and variety of services will keep even rapidly-expanding Tucson commercially subservient to a considerable degree. To the east, El Paso and Albuquerque divide most of the remainder between them, with El Paso's considerably larger wholesale trade reflecting its special reach into northern Mexico as well. In the southeast, the local commerce is shared among the several cities of which Roswell is the largest, but to a considerable degree the area, and especially the Clovis-Hobbs border zone of Little Texas, is more closely tied to Amarillo, Lubbock, and Fort Worth than to Albuquerque or El Paso.

In recent years, the pattern and frequency of scheduled air service within the region is an important indicator of commercial relations, although by its nature it reveals more how the several main centers are linked together than how each is bound to its main trade area. By this measure Albuquerque appears as the principal regional focus, having non-stop service to nine cities within the Southwest and being the hub of a wider network of direct service than any other. But air service is also a useful indicator of the ties between the region and the nation within an ever more important dimension of the over-all circulation network. In this, Phoenix is clearly pre-eminent, the power of its size and functions giving it non-stop service to sixteen cities beyond the Southwest, including the only such regional link with New York City. Albuquerque ranks second, an expression of its position as the eastern gateway to the Southwest for service from the Middle West and East. The more limited connections of El Paso and Tucson reflect in part the barrier of the border; the fact that Tucson has non-stop service to Chicago while El Paso has such eastward service only to Texas cities is an expression of the difference between a national desert playground and a regional industrial center.

Much of the traffic moving along all of these various routes has of course always been simply an expression of the particular location of the Southwest within the nation, and the railroads and highways and air lanes have functioned more as segments of a national system than as parts of a discrete regional network. Such a relative location has therefore been unusually important to the regional economy, but it has been perhaps even more important to regional demography. For to be on the routeways to California has meant being continuously washed by the most powerful interregional tides of population movement on the continent. And while millions have moved across this Southwest, hundreds of thousands have come to stay, with marked effect upon the regional social geography.

8 DEMOGRAPHIC AND POLITICAL

PATTERNS: 1900-1970

Numbers and Peoples

In 1970 the Southwest had a little more than three million people. That represented a ninefold increase since 1900 but left it still a relatively thinly populated American region. (Fig. 8-1) Texas, only slightly larger in area, had more than three times as many people; California, a third smaller, had six times as many. Such a difference from such neighbors is of course hardly surprising given the physical conditions of this largely arid or semi-arid country. What is more remarkable is the fact that the Southwest has recently become one of the fastest growing regions in the nation, having nearly doubled in population in the last twenty years. That mighty spurt of growth followed a long period of only modest annual increments and was the most obvious indication of the new era of development following World War II. Inevitably all such growth, large or small, was unevenly proportioned among the various areas and several components of the population and thus has produced some major modifications in the social and political geography of the region. (Fig. 8-2)

Although every county has felt the touch of this general regional growth at some time during these seven decades, some have felt it only very lightly, and a few only very briefly or intermittently. Mining camps of course were notoriously unstable in prosperity and the fluctuation of the population totals of several counties is directly attributable to such economic instability. The dry-farming areas of northeast New Mexico

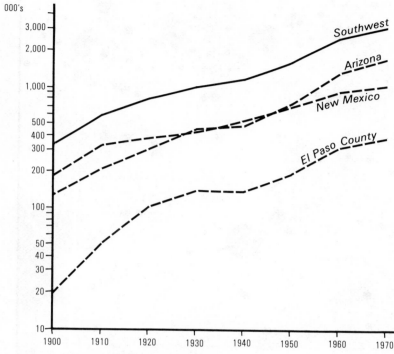

FIG. 8-1. Population Growth, 1900-1970

show a simpler pattern of change: a quick increase early in the century and a slow persistent decline until today that corner holds little more than half the population it did in 1910. More recently the back-country of the old Rio Arriba area has shown a similar decline.

Southeastern New Mexico, in contrast, has been an area of continuous and at times vigorous growth. Between 1910 and 1940, the five counties which approximate the area of "Little Texas" doubled in population and then doubled again in twenty years to constitute a quarter of the state's total population, a fact of major social and political significance. Northwestern New Mexico experienced about the same sequence of growth with a smaller population, with the sudden expansions of Farmington and Grants being rather similar to those of Hobbs and Carlsbad. Elsewhere—in addition to the almost explosive expansion of Albuquerque—Las Cruces, Alamogordo, and Los Alamos are important new growth points in the state. The last is much more significant than just that, of course, for it represents a wholly new kind of community

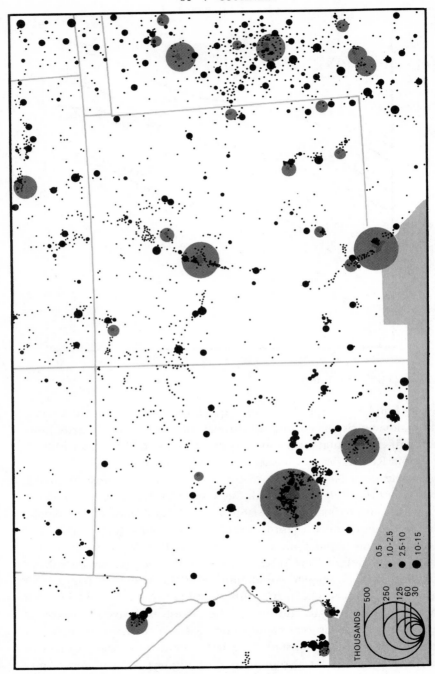

FIG. 8-2. Population Distribution, 1960

composed almost entirely of scientists and administrators and their families, a national elite in education, income, and prestige. Similar people are now an important, if somewhat less visible, element in the citizenry of Albuquerque, Santa Fe, and Alamogordo, and not only have they had a major impact upon their communities but they represent, in total, a new, distinctive, relatively homogeneous component of the state's population which has a significance far greater than its numbers.

Over-all, central Arizona, with the most varied and powerful combination of growth factors, has been by far the most important subregion of demographic change. Since 1900 Phoenix and the Gila-Salt River oasis have accounted for more than 30 per cent of the total population increase in the Southwest.

The particular qualities of the area led to the development of some distinctive settlements quite early in the century. Chandler, though rather more elegant in style than most, was a good illustration of one kind. It was founded in 1912 by Dr. A. J. Chandler who was faced with the fact that under federal regulations water from the new Roosevelt Dam could be brought to his 18,000-acre ranch only if the land was subdivided and sold in units no larger than 160 acres. Therefore he had all the irrigable land laid out in small farm blocks and hired a California architect to design a town that would be "the Pasadena of the Salt River Valley." To help establish the desired tone at the outset, Dr. Chandler built the San Marcos Hotel, a California Mission style resort occupying the entire west side of the central plaza, and all the town was carefully zoned to ensure qualities and uses appropriate to the general plan. The whole scheme was a general success, the town of Chandler proved a lure to settler, sojourner, and tourist alike, for its was at once a pleasant and prosperous place in which to live, a resort to relax in, and a sight to see.

Another type of carefully planned and nurtured settlement was the company town of Litchfield Park, laid out by the Goodyear Company in 1917 in the midst of lands it had leased to develop the production of long-staple cotton for use in its new cord tires. More common were those towns, such as Guadalupe and Tolleson, which simply grew to be almost entirely dormitory towns for the large numbers of laborers in the surrounding fields—agricultural counterparts of the industrial workers' towns in the mining camps. Such towns were relatively early representatives of the specialized settlements amidst the more common trade centers.

But all of these centers are in some degree no more than suburbs or satellites of Phoenix which, over the span of these seventy years has grown from a town of five thousand to a sprawling city of half a million people. As such, Phoenix is simply the outstanding exhibit of the emergence of a metropolitanism which now dominates the thinly populated Southwest as surely as other regions of the nation. Here it is a quite recent phenomenon. In 1900 El Paso with only 16,000 people was much the largest city and, together with Albuquerque, Phoenix, and Tucson, contained only 10 per cent of the regional population; today those four cities contain about half of the total. Since World War II the growth in the four counties containing these four metropolises has accounted for nearly three-quarters of the total increment to the regional population. Furthermore, the difference in scale between these large cities and those next in size (Roswell, with 40,000 is the next largest) is now clearly a difference in kind as well as degree, between truly metropolitan centers and no more than small cities. Such differences seem likely to be magnified for some time to come.

The various streams of immigration which have powered so much of this growth have had marked effects upon the composition of the population. Throughout these seventy years the American Middle West has been consistently the most important source region, with Texas and Oklahoma a strong second, California third, and Mexico intermittently significant. Although California has been a large contributor, it has also been a strong competitor and in some decades it drew more Southwest residents on west than it sent its own east. Arizona, especially, has clearly been no more than a way-station for many thousands of newcomers who after a sojourn of a few seasons move on to the ultimate West. In a rather less transient way, close ties of family and business sustain a good deal of migration to as well as from Texas, especially from southern and eastern New Mexico.

The several corridors of immigration have become much less sharply identified with particular peoples, chiefly because with the colonization of western Texas and Oklahoma, and the development of Routes 66 and 84, migrants from those states moved along the Northern as well as the Southern Corridor, and also because of the increasingly strong pull and easy accessibility of various centers along the southern route for migrants from anywhere who seek the special amenities of warm desert living. Those amenities continue to be the region's most powerful lure. In a recent survey of a cross section of Arizona immigrants, half cited climate and health as the major reason for their move. Yet only a small proportion of these were invalids or retired people; they came seeking jobs in a more congenial physical environment, a congeniality, it should be mentioned, which is in part a relatively recent product of man for it is only the widespread use of air-conditioning that makes the desert sun more than a winter pleasure.

Early in the century foreign-born migrants from southern and eastern Europe were a small but rather distinctive element in the movements from the East and Middle West. Italians, Slavs, and Greeks were prominent in the populations of the coal towns and railroad towns along the Northern Corridor but in total did not add very significantly to the heterogeneity of the regional population.

A much more visible and increasingly important element of these westward migrations has been the native Black American. Although Negroes have been present in the Southwest about as long as Anglos, they have constituted no more than a small infiltration until quite recently. By 1940 they numbered about 22,000, less than 2 per cent of the regional total; twenty years later there were 70,000, which made them only a slightly higher proportion but a sufficient number to be a significant component in certain areas. As an integral part of the westward tides of Texan and Southern migrations, coming as laborers and settling in areas of strong Southern influence, they remained locked in a segregated society. Until very recently, Negroes faced routine discrimination in public facilities as well as residential areas all over Little Texas and along the Southern Corridor. In Phoenix, for example, public schools, hotels, restaurants, theaters, and swimming pools were segregated—evidence of the firm impress of Southern racial mores upon what its spokesmen like to claim as the "all-American" city of the Southwest.

The Oriental population, a few thousand Chinese, Japanese, and Filipinos, is a tiny but complementary exhibit of a racial component peculiar to the eastward migrations. For Arizona (where most of them have lived) early imitated California in barring or expelling the Chinese from some of the mining camps and later in passing state laws to prohibit the Japanese from owning farm land. In 1942 several of the concentration camps for the Japanese-Americans expelled from the Pacific Coast were established in the Arizona desert.

El Paso and Nogales have been the main portals for Mexican migrations into the region. Although such people have spread very widely over the western United States, in this sector the great majority have settled very near the border. In 1960 more than half of the total population of "Mexican stock" (that is, Mexican-born or with at least one Mexican-born parent) still clung to the immediate border localities of El Paso-Mesilla Valley, Douglas, Bisbee, Nogales, and Yuma. Most of the remainder were in the Tucson and Phoenix areas. It is important to note that northern New Mexico, which might seem superficially to hold a kindred population, attracted few such immigrants in the twentieth century. The fact that in 1960 Albuquerque, the great growth center of that area, had fewer than 4000 persons of such "Mexican stock" compared with 40,000 in the Phoenix area and 95,000 in El Paso County illustrates how shallow in penetration this important migration has been in this region. Such geographic distributions reinforced and sustained the general separation discernible at the beginning of the century between this Mexican-American population and the historic Hispano peoples of northern New Mexico: the one a recent, rather transient proletariat concentrated in the industrial camps of mining and agriculture with still strong cultural and familial ties across the border; the other an isolated, closely knit, and deeply rooted peasantry.

It is this latter group, the native Hispano peoples of New Mexico, which has felt most heavily the impact of these various migrations. Sometime in the 1930's the cumulative immigration of Anglos had reduced the proportionate position of the Hispanos to but half of the total population of the state. In the 1960's they made up less than 30 per cent in the state and the huge Anglo influx to Albuquerque, Santa Fe, and Los Alamos had even left them a minority group within their own immediate homeland. (Fig. 8-3)

The relative position of the Indians has been even more drastically altered, reduced from 12 per cent of the total population in 1900 to about 5 per cent. However, such a decline in proportion masked a notable increase in actual numbers—from about 40,000 to perhaps 150,-000, a recovery which represents a reinvigoration of Indian societies to a degree utterly unexpected earlier in the century. The great majority have remained at least legally resident within their reservations, although an ever-increasing number hold at least seasonal jobs outside. Of the several tribes, the Navaho, numbering nearly 100,000, is much the largest (indeed much the largest in the United States as well) and most rapidly growing, a reflection of the Navaho's remarkable ability to adapt to the pressures and opportunities arising from enforced contacts with American society and at the same time to maintain the basic integrity and spirit of their own culture. The 20,000 Pueblo Indians

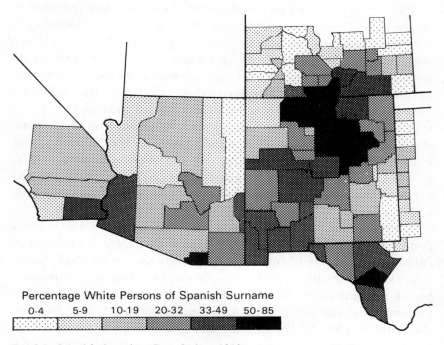

Percentage White Persons of Spanish Surname

| 0-4 | 5-9 | 10-19 | 20-32 | 33-49 | 50-85 |

FIG. 8-3. Spanish-American Population, 1960

continued their even more persistent record of such accommodation without assimilation. Although all tribes now live under even more comprehensive, if somewhat less brutal, pressures from the encompassing national society, the quiet determination and power of the Indians to remain a people apart are ever more evident; and despite the decline in their proportionate strength they remain so clearly a significant population in several large areas as to help sustain the distinctive multi-cultural character of the Southwest.

POLITICAL GEOGRAPHY

The formal political geography of the region was elaborated and stabilized during these years. The defeat of the statehood proposal of 1890 only prolonged the issue and encouraged further complex maneuvers in the territories and in Congress. The most radical proposal to emerge was that of "jointure"—the admission of Arizona and New Mexico as a single state. Such a bill was very nearly approved by Congress in 1905 but in its last stages was amended to require a local referendum on the issue. For a variety of reasons the Anglo-Hispano leadership in New Mexico had by this time decided to support statehood and, if necessary, jointure. But all of the Arizona Anglo interests viewed the single-state idea as abhorrent, a forced "miscegenation" of their "American" territory with a despotic Hispano-Catholic land, and thus when the question was put to a vote New Mexicans narrowly approved (probably with the help of fraudulent counts), and Arizonans soundly rejected, the idea. With that concept of political unity for the Southwest dead, statehood for each territory was revived, and after seven more years of political maneuvers was finally approved in 1912, confirming the geographical design which had served as the gross political framework for half a century.

Statehood could only win support in New Mexico if the Hispano population was assured of protection against the power of the national culture. Thus the state constitution contains many provisions specifically assuring equality of rights regardless of race, language, or religion, prohibiting any forced public segregation of Hispano peoples, and at the same time sustaining them in the maintenance of their language and culture. Thus by law New Mexico was bilingual in schools and public life. Furthermore such initial safeguards have had the vigorous support of an alert and influential electorate. For the Hispanos of northern New Mexico have not been at all the politically impassive proletariat manipulated by an Anglo minority as has been so common in neighboring parts of the United States, but rather a full society with a very high level of political participation and often very capable political leadership, though, as well, a society so riven by internal factions as to reduce its actual power.

While the Hispanos have thus ever been joint rulers of their state, their declining proportion of the total population has gradually eroded their traditional power. As new counties were created in response to the spread of new populations into certain areas, that formal political framework became increasingly expressive of the underlying patterns of social geography. As measured by nominations and elections, New Mexican counties could be classified into three general groups: very strongly Hispano, very strongly Anglo, and a fairly balanced mixture of the two. Until the 1930's the Hispanos were very largely Republican, and the Anglos of the east and south were very largely Democratic, and thus the regional pattern of peoples was a rather direct reflection of patterns of political power. The fact that by the 1930's these three groups of counties were very nearly equal in total population meant that state-wide and national political life in New Mexico was critically dependent upon the delicate working relationships between Anglos and Hispanos in a few counties, and especially in Bernalillo (Albuquerque). Such a role for this locality was but a modern political expression of its historic pivotal position in the cultural geography of the Southwest, the principal crossroads where the westward moving Anglos had cut through the old Hispano axis. It was thus important not simply because it contained the largest city, but because it also contained one of the longest histories as a place of sustained and reasonably balanced cultural contact. That gave it a strategic political role even greater than its commercial one, for it served the entire state as chief mediator of the stark cultural contrasts and latent animosities between the solidly Hispano and tradition-bound core of old Rio Arriba and the new aggressive and solidly Anglo creation of Little Texas on the high flatlands of the eastern border. (Fig. 8-4)

The trends of the last thirty years have inevitably altered these patterns. The transformation of Albuquerque from a small city into a metropolis has made it less a mediator than a dominator. In the 1960's, Bernalillo County alone became the largest subregional political area in New Mexico; in 1964 it cast 30 per cent of the total state vote in the gubernatorial contest, more than all the other "most Hispano" counties combined. The Hispano counties and Little Texas still constitute recognizable political regions within the state but each is rather less tradition-bound and cohesive. Indeed, each has actually shifted its predominant political affiliation: since the New Deal in the 1930's the Hispanos have become increasingly Democratic, while the prosperous and ideologically conservative electorate of Little Texas has become preponderantly Republican at the national level. In contrast, the voters of Bernalillo County, now 80 per cent Anglo and mostly new to the state, display all the political inconstancies of the new middle-class urban South and West, uncohesive and almost apolitical much of the time, but sharply responsive to particular issues and national moods, and generally more conservative than the urban voters in the Northeast.

There has been nothing comparable in Arizona to these special complexities of New Mexico. The state constitution of 1912 was unusual only in its close reflection of some current national movements

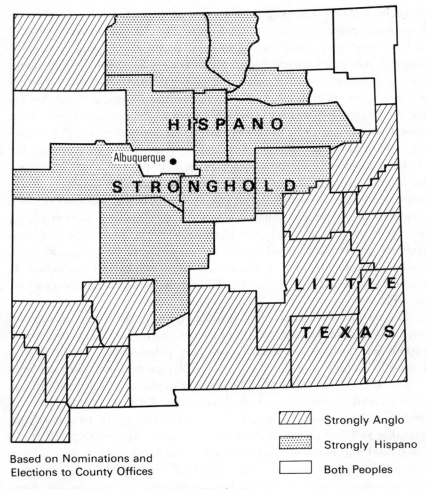

Based on Nominations and
Elections to County Offices

Strongly Anglo

Strongly Hispano

Both Peoples

FIG. 8-4. Political Regionalism (New Mexico)

rather than of local peculiarities, for it incorporated some of the newer
devices of democratic government (especially initiative, referendum, and
recall) which had been advocated during the Progressive Era of the new
century. Nor has there been anything approaching the political sec-
tionalism of New Mexico. The strength of the Democratic party into the
1950's was certainly in part a reflection of the continual inflow of Southern immigrants, but the state has never had a "Little Texas" and the
party has been a fluid amalgam of such varied groups as traditional
Democratic Southerners, industrial laborers (mostly Mexican-American),

and reform-minded citizens, which for a time proved so successful in elections as to win continued support from others who sought to influence legislation. But party affiliation has never been strong and politics has never been a really intense concern in Arizona. Its citizens have been too detached from former homelands and too shallow in their local roots to express traditional reactions, too removed from exacerbating deep-seated issues to be intensely concerned, too changeable in numbers and residence to provide a stable base for professional political cliques.

The great inflow of people since World War II has had an effect on the political climate of Arizona by strongly accentuating a more self-conscious ideological conservatism, a local trend given national prominence in the candidacy of Barry Goldwater in 1964. The unusually large vote cast in Arizona for the Republican presidential candidate in that year was of course in part an expression of pride in a famous member of a highly respected family long resident in the state, but the ideology he represented, the most conservative stance taken by a major national party in many years, has become the dominant force in Arizona. As strongly supported by new industrialists, small business proprietors, suburban home owners, and retirees, as by the older ranching interests, it is very much a political reflection of the selectivity of migration and subsequent prosperity in a highly dynamic Southwestern society.

For the region as a whole, therefore, the most obvious general trend is toward the increasing dominance of politically conservative Anglos, an association of demographic and political processes which is characteristic of much of the entire western half of the nation. Such processes, as well as those associated with economic developments and transportation improvements, are all part of the ever closer integration and assimilation of the region into the body of the nation. Nevertheless, in 1970 this Southwest was far from being a typical Western region, and there were signs that warned against any simple projection of apparently dominant trends toward its becoming such. For not only was its remarkable cultural diversity still readily visible, there were political indications that the social significance of its minority peoples would be greater in the late than in the early twentieth century. The remarkable, incendiary activities of radical Hispano organizations in Rio Arriba, the slow but relentless program to organize and politicize the *chicanos* of the border counties, the restlessness of Black Americans in Phoenix, the emergence of political sophistication and activism among American Indians (a national movement which logically must seek to establish its main base in this very region), these and related movements are at once reflections of broader radical developments in the nation at large and responses to the constrictions and pressures felt very directly at home. Although no more than minor tremors as yet, they tell of the deep-seated and probably increasing tensions laid down over the course of the peculiar social history and expressing the peculiar social geography of this Southwest.

9 REGIONAL SOCIAL

GEOGRAPHY, c. 1970

In the latter part of the twentieth century as at its beginning, every generalization about the Southwest as a region requires explication in terms of subregions. The same general diversity of parts identified for 1900 is still recognizable but each is sufficiently altered in content and significance to give a different configuration to the whole.

NORTHERN NEW MEXICO

Logically, because of the position of the Southwest in relation to the rest of the country, most travelers enter by land or by air by way of its northeastern corner, the oldest Anglo entryway. The visitor is thereby brought into that part which has been most extensively celebrated by regional authors and advertisers as the most "colorful country," rich in its varieties of man and nature, and in its tangible layers of history. It is a variety to be encountered on the streets of its cities: Indians and Hispanos, artists and authors, "hippie" idealists or escapists and health-seekers, atomic physicists and anthropologists, ranchers and resort owners, priests and nuns and itinerant evangelists. It is a variety expressed in language, dress, and behavior—a variety as apparent in some parts of the countryside as in the city, where the near juxtaposition of *kiva, morada,* churches, chapel and store-front sect indicates half a dozen sub-societies sharing a single valley. It is a richness of history expressed in the continuous occupancy of thirteenth-century pueblos, in the historical sequence of styles displayed in the conglomerate of city archi-

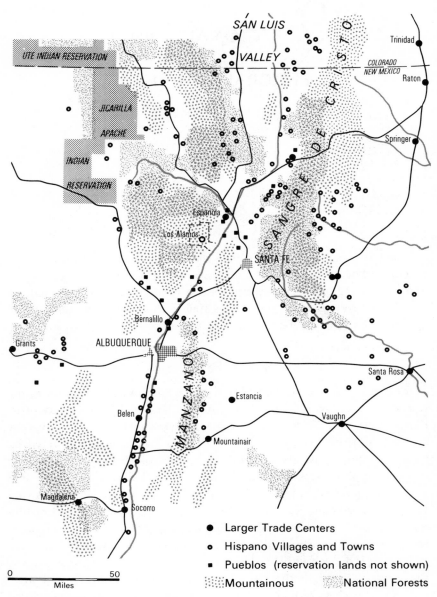

Larger Trade Centers

Hispano Villages and Towns

Pueblos (reservation lands not shown)

Mountainous   National Forests

0   50
Miles

FIG. 9-1. Northern New Mexico

tecture, in the fact that life today goes on amidst the ruins of the richest archeological landscape in the nation.

In general, the social geography of the area might be characterized as old Hispano country encompassing the rigid compartments of Pueblo lands and riddled by Anglo intrusions. (Fig. 9-1 & 9-2) It extends from above San Luis, Colorado, to below Socorro, New Mexico, embracing the whole breadth of the mountain country in the North from the upper waters of the Canadian to those of the San Juan, tapering southward to include the Manzano Range, but now contracted on the west by the abandonment of the Rio Puerco country made virtually uninhabitable by decades of overgrazing and flash flooding.

Albuquerque and Santa Fe, in a very real sense joint capitals as in so many American states, the one the commercial focus the other the political focus, lie near the center of this subregion and, despite a special importance and flavor of the rural scene, here as elsewhere in our metropolitan age these two cities provide the most appropriate introduction to some of the most important characteristics of the general area.

Both of these cities and their environs clearly exhibit the three peoples, Indian, Hispano, and Anglo, but they do so in quite different ways, for upon closer look each is a mirror of its own particular portion of this historic core area of New Mexico. Today those portions are sufficiently different as to suggest the revival of the old terms *Rio Abajo* and *Rio Arriba* as a useful means of referring to these areas of more local contrast, the one exhibiting what appears to be a strong trend of the future, the other the still firm hold of the past.

The over-all form and character of Albuquerque display the rapid and relentless increase in Anglo dominance of what has long been the largest city in this old Pueblo-Hispano realm. The old depot-plaza axis which so well expressed the original Anglo-Hispano balance and connection is still discernible but it now has little symbolic or functional importance as such. Those old terminals are now a tourist focus at the west end and a little-used railroad station and hotel at the east. Today the most obvious instance of an Old Town-New Town contrast lies not in the historic pattern peculiar to the region but in the modern pattern so common in the nation: between the pre-1945 city focused on its central business district and the sprawling postwar outer growth of highway commercial strips, shopping centers, and new tract residential areas, a development which appears to have had a strongly depressant effect upon the older Albuquerque. The pseudo-pueblo style of various buildings, and especially of the expanding university, sustains the gesture of interest in regional cultural antecedents, but the parking lot plazas, new one-story business strips, garish standardized chain-store service stops, and the towering glitter of glass and steel office buildings attest to the far greater power of an aggressive national culture.

Although there are some 50,000 Hispanos in Albuquerque they now make up less than a quarter of the population. They are mostly an urban laboring class living in the older areas of the valley floor, but they have long been sufficiently numerous to support a considerable number of their own kind in businesses and professions, and their residential clusters are probably more the result of income levels and social choice than of systematic cultural discrimination in real estate. Moreover, there is much evidence of their economic progress and modern acculturation, as, for example, in the block after block of neat little houses and lawns on little rectangular plots—a kind of plain and miniature version of national ranchhouse suburbia far removed from the stone or adobe casa-corrals of their local ancestors.

Many of the most obvious marks of the dominant culture—supermarkets and service stations, used car lots and drive-in restaurants—are evident through the whole length of Rio Abajo, but in some of the smaller towns and villages they still seem discordant. Hispano and Anglo farms and homes are closely intermingled along the main highway of this riverine strip in all the gradations in quality from crumbling shacks to expensive ranchhouses, yet though these two people to a large extent live side by side, work together, and intermingle daily to form a general public, they still tend to live much of their lives as separate subsocieties. In the more intimate matters of worship and marriage, eating and drinking, visiting and playing, the members of each group strongly tend to stick with their own kind and thereby to sustain many de facto separate facilities despite little overtly coercive segregation.

In the lee of the mountains east of Albuquerque the two poples are more separated in area and in prospects. It would be hard to find a harsher contrast than that between the prosperous Anglos vigorously expanding into new housing tracts in the Sandias and the depleted impoverished Hispano population twenty miles to the south in the decaying villages along the foot of the Manzanos.

Amidst that jumble along the main highway which runs parallel to the Rio Grande are the pueblos of Sandia and Isleta, whose mud-plastered houses, bare earthen plazas, and disheveled brush fences seem

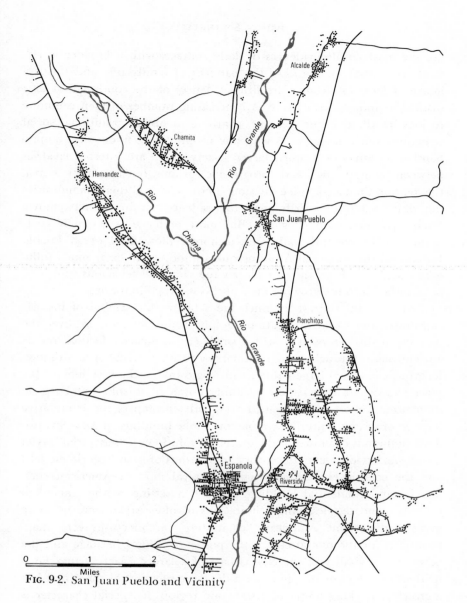

Alcalde

Chamita

Rio Grande

Hernandez

Rio

Chama

San Juan Pueblo

Rio Grande

Ranchitos

Espanola

Riverside

0   1   2
Miles

FIG. 9-2. San Juan Pueblo and Vicinity

an especially striking contrast to the modern American urban forms near by. But these ancient villages are not fading relics; they are viable centers of a people who have maintained a basic cultural identity. They are at once integral functioning parts of this greater metropolitan complex and remarkable social enclaves, insulated in many ways from the metropolitan swirl. Television aerials, automobiles, and pickup trucks are the most visible evidences of daily contacts with a broader world, while the rituals of the *kiva,* the patterns of family life, and the language of local intercourse are firm evidences of the continuation of a distinctive indigenous culture. An increasing number of men commute to jobs in Albuquerque, yet they continue to sustain traditional social structures and ideologies. As with any people living under the comprehensive pressures of a much larger society, there are internal rivalries between "conservative" and "progressive" groups, but it is more a creative tension than a corrosive division. Those who find their communities too rigid and insular drift away to residence within the city, moves often associated with exogamy. But most prefer to keep their roots within their ancestral walls and, although these 2000 or so Pueblo Indians on the fringes of Albuquerque are too few to exert much influence upon the whole, they are clearly too vital and tenacious simply to be absorbed into the growing mass of this metropolitan area.

Santa Fe, in contrast, is much more the visible symbol of historic continuity and social integration. Despite a doubling in size over the past twenty-five years, it is still a small city compactly focused on its ancient plazas through a tangle of narrow turning streets. And although its growth has been largely due to an Anglo influx, the very look of the place everywhere shows the continuing power of Pueblo and Hispano influences. Almost any extended view will encompass the cumulative imprint of several centuries: simple low adobe buildings of early Spanish days; numerous examples of the graceful evolutionary "territorial" style; a wide variety of twentieth-century adaptations of such historic models; and the eclectic expressions of more typical modern American commercial and residential building. In such a setting neither the more contrived and tasteless Anglo imitations of older styles nor the more garishly discordant American "chain-store" architecture seem inappropriate, for the one attests to the power of a local heritage and the other to the vitality of the city as part of a larger society. Santa Fe is neither a mere museum piece nor a decaying remnant of times past but a growing, working center of a state and region. Its special character is basically genuine, for it is a direct reflection of its hinterland, and it is further self-sustaining in that, devoid of large industries, it attracts primarily those Anglo migrants who seek its special environmental qualities. The variety and complexity of its architecture are reflections of the diversity of its intermingled peoples.

In part, this expression of continuity and integration reflects its role for more than three and a half centuries as a capital city, through Spanish, Mexican, American territorial, and statehood eras, a function bringing these various peoples into a necessary working relationship at this point. In part, it reflects its equally lengthy role as the unchallenged focus of Rio Arriba, the stronghold of Pueblo and Hispano peoples with long a powerful attraction for particular kinds of Anglos.

There are eight pueblos within thirty miles of Santa Fe, some of them now quite small but all of them very active centers of Pueblo culture. Here, as downriver, is to be seen a pattern of life which partakes of two social worlds but remains firmly anchored in one. The Pueblo breadwinner may drive a new car to a job in Los Alamos, buy cement blocks to enlarge his house, cultivate the family plot with a tractor, and watch national television programs every evening, but his roots remain deep in ancestral ground and his social behavior remains strongly shaped by traditional influences. From infancy he has spoken a Pueblo tongue, he will almost certainly marry a Pueblo girl, and he will very likely participate in a rich annual cycle of religious and social observances. He is thus a full member of a highly localized community which, even though riven with internal factions, remains cohesive against the highly aggressive and powerful society which encompasses it.

An important factor in the maintenance of such communal integrity was the ultimate confirmation by the American government of Pueblo title to most of their ancestral cultivated lands. It was a long political and legal process which involved the forced recovery of many land parcels from non-Indian users to create a contiguous reservation around or adjacent to each Pueblo village, a formal inviolable girdle reinforcing the cultural insularity. But this belated success of the Indians generated a deep resentment in their immediate neighbors. For most lands restored to the Pueblos were taken from local Hispanos who had acquired them as bits and pieces in common ways over a long period of time. Such land is as fundamental to the one group as to the other, is used in generally similar ways for similar purposes. Furthermore, both peoples were captives of American rule and were ostensibly protected in their land rights by treaties and constitutions, yet both had suffered from severe encroachments by the invading Anglos. Therefore, to have the national government restore long lost lands to the one people and not to the other—and often worse, to take directly from the one to benefit the other—could only seem to the Hispanos an outrageous discrimination against them. Such a policy not only further embittered the

Hispanos against the Anglo government but did much to foster a social separation between these two local peoples so long closely associated.

It is one of the most fundamental features of the region that, although many thousands more numerous than the Indians, it is the Hispanos who show the greater stress of culture contact. They make up at least two-thirds of the population in the mountain country to the north and to the east of Santa Fe and the entire population of many of its tiny villages, but the power of their numbers is undercut by the debilitation of their economy and culture. Though they appear to be the dominant people in the landscape they are a rural population with little land, a labor force with little work to do, isolated physically and socially from the main streams of national life yet exposed enough to feel many of its pressures. Clustered in ramshackle half-empty villages of adobe, stone, and rusting iron roofs, often ill-clothed, ill-fed, and unschooled (a large proportion has been well described as "illiterate in two languages"), they have become a society obsessed with politics as a means of sustenance, with welfare payments, pensions, and patronage shoring up a desperately deficient local economy.

Some of those deficiencies can be read in the face of the land itself almost anywhere along the upper Rio Grande, the Chama, the Pecos, the Mora, or nearby valleys: small, discontinuous riverine terraces minutely subdivided among too many families; tiny inadequately irrigated patches of corn, beans, and chili peppers; unkempt insect-ridden orchards; little corrals with a few head of low-grade livestock; surrounded by eroded slopes and barren mesas veneered with all the tell-tale scars of chronic overgrazing; and, in any extended view, some sign of the relentless encroachment of outside forces: a national forest boundary marking the limits of uncontrolled use, a seasonal recreation facility for affluent Anglos—dude ranch, hunting lodge, children's summer camp, or ski slope—or, most commonly, the isolated dwelling be it a modern "ranchhouse" or an aluminum "mobile home," of an Anglo escaping from the city or suburbia of his own kind.

The relative poverty of most of the Hispanos in Rio Arriba is starkly apparent. What is not immediately obvious is the fact that the plight of those now living in the area would be much worse without the help received from those who have left. The export of labor from this backcountry is as old as Anglo development near by, but what started as a regional use of traditional skills—herding for the Anglo rancher, freighting for the Anglo merchant—soon became simply an industrial use of cheap labor far afield in alien country: in the sugarbeet fields of Colorado, the steel mills of Pueblo, the packing houses of Kansas City, in the railroad gangs spaced along the lines from Albuquerque to Chicago. Thus for at least the past fifty years most of these little villages which seem so self-contained, insulated, and discordant from modern America have actually been ever more critically bound to the nation through kinfolk who have scattered over half the continent forming little enclaves of reluctant expatriates caught in the web of the industrial-metropolitan system.

And, of course, even those little plazas tucked deeply in the arroyos and canyons and folds of the mountains are not very isolated anymore. Electricity has been brought to nearly every one, the roads are improved bit by bit, year by year, and radio and television are everywhere a common and important part of daily life. Yet despite extensive acculturation and participation in modern society there remains a quiet stubborn adherence to language, religion, and many folkways. The persistence of the Penitentes and the sudden emergence of the Alianza are only the more spectacular evidences that these Hispanos, no less than their Pueblo neighbors, are an American minority which steadfastly insists on an alternative to full assimilation into a national culture.

Thus if Santa Fe and the Rio Arriba continue to offer the most colorful and extensive display of cultural variety and history in the Southwest and continue to attract in ever greater numbers settlers, sojourners, and tourists who are fascinated by such features, it is important to realize that it is likewise the most crisis-ridden area in the Southwest, uneasy with the tensions arising from the very vividness of that cultural variety and from the pride and the fear accumulated over that long history.

CENTRAL ARIZONA

Although central Arizona is in general the obvious counterpart of northern New Mexico, the chief focus of the western half of that broad Gila-Rio Grande dualism of the Southwest as herein defined, the contrasts in the character of these two areas, whether viewed broadly or in detail, seem far more striking than any similarities. For central Arizona is essentially one vast metropolitan structure, an intricate, intensive compound of residential, recreational, commercial, industrial, and agricultural parts bound together in one contiguous sprawling oasis. Beyond

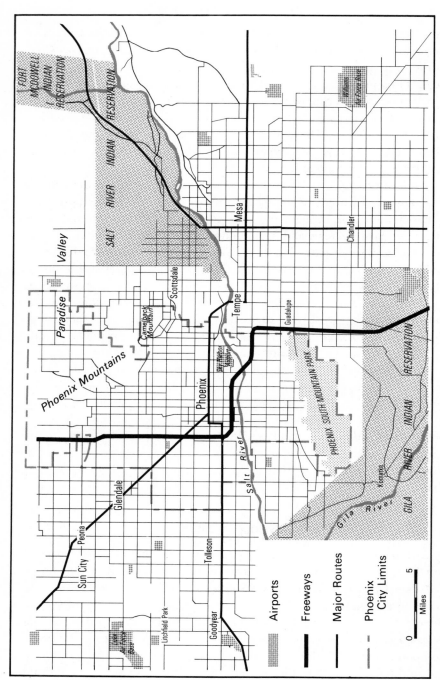

Fig. 9-3. Central Arizona

the ever-changing edge of this dense web lies not a rural backcountry of isolated derelict villages but desert and mountain country dotted with modern dude ranches and other resorts, all specialized outliers tied closely to this urban system by private planes and high-speed highways. Furthermore, there is little obvious evidence of history in this dynamic metropolitan scene. Some of its constituent settlements were founded a century ago but none was very large until quite recently. Further, so much of the landscape has been formed in the last decade or two as to make the entire complex seem like an almost instant modern creation. And despite the presence of four peoples, central Arizona has essentially but one culture. For the Indians, though as deeply rooted here as in New Mexico, are a tiny minority living mostly along the fringe, and neither the Spanish- nor the Black Americans are products of the local region but migrant peoples who have been drawn in by the influx of Anglos. Lured as a labor force, they have found homes in the older parts of the Anglo towns and are completely bound to and largely imitative of the dominant Anglo culture.

This generally contiguous metropolitan complex stretches for over fifty miles, elongated to the northwest and southeast across the usually dry bed of the Salt River, constricted in the middle by mountains and Indian reservations, fanning out to broad edges of growth on the west and east. (Fig. 9-3) In part it has been formed by a coalescence of separate growing towns, in part by gradual outward expansion. Nearly the entire area is laid out in a rigid grid set square with the cardinal points in typical American fashion. Within the basic framework of square-mile blocks there are still scattered areas of open fields, groves, and barren spaces held on speculation, but the pressures for more intensive use of land are rapidly bringing about subdivision and development, with a consequent progress toward uniform density. Downtown Phoenix is near the actual midpoint of central Arizona and serves as the most important cluster of its kind, though this sprawling metropolitan unit has no clearly dominant nucleus. The central business district of Phoenix is but one among many and is by no means the most attractive retail area. Even the state capitol provides little urban focus.

Such dispersal, such extensive decentralization of common functions is, of course, the common form of a metropolis created in the automobile age, and all the other marks are readily apparent: broad streets, low business blocks, single houses on spacious lots, commercial strips, huge shopping plazas, and drive-in facilities of every conceivable type. It is an urban form and a style of life most commonly associated with southern California and its emergence here in central Arizona is a product of generally similar environment, activities, and people, and to some extent of the direct influence of Californian capital and entrepreneurs.

Within this general whole there are of course some marked differences among the parts, differences in people, wealth, and functions which give an individuality to various localities. Among the more prominent are Tempe and Mesa, relatively old towns of entirely modern mien; in Tempe the old state normal school has been transformed into a large university, in Mesa the Mormon Temple serves as a religious focus for the 40,000 or so members of that faith now residing in the valley. Scottsdale, with its controlled, contrived "western" architecture and the large residential estates to the north with their conspicuous displays of wealth, contrasts sharply with the Negro and Spanish-American sections of south Phoenix and with agricultural laborer towns such as Tolleson and the Yaqui Indian community of Guadalupe. The San Marcos Hotel still dominates the plaza at Chandler, and the obvious prosperity of the town attests to the success of Dr. Chandler's program of carefully planned development, which became the general model for many others. At the western edge of the metropolis the Goodyear Company now has under way a master plan for the controlled sequential transformation of much of its cotton lands into a dozen villages which eventually will form an integrated city. Just to the north, Sun City, a completely planned retirement community, is but the most elaborate of several similar projects in the area.

Expansion continues vigorously to the east and west and sporadically along the highway far to the northwest, where little tracts of new houses stand starkly in the desert. On the south, the Gila River Indian Reservation blocks extension, and the Pima villages along the river offer the sharpest contrast to the general scene to be found anywhere in the region. Beyond, separated from the main metropolitan web by the empty expanse of the reservation, lies the still largely agricultural triangle of Coolidge-Casa Grande-Eloy.

It is generally assumed that there are rather severe limits to continued outward expansion in this desert, but it is not at all clear just where such limits may be. Water continues to be made available; its cost may rise, but that does not loom as a deterrent, and there are large supplies latent in more efficient distribution and use. The conversion of land from agriculture still offers simple and relatively inexpensive access to space and water for other developments. Only a very small portion of the commercial and residential land is now under what by national standards would be considered intensive use. There are now about a million people in this contiguous metropolitan complex and there appears to be no reason, local or national, not to expect in the next decade what has happened in the last two: the average yearly addition of 30,000 people.

The combination of attractions, physical, economic, and social, seems undiminished in its power. Reductions in the demand for agricultural labor are more than offset by continually increasing needs for unskilled and semi-skilled workers in industrial and municipal service. The fact that so many people seek the area for other than economic reasons continues to attract a wide variety of corporations which have found that just such people make unusually contented employees. Thus in the latter twentieth century, central Arizona stands as one of the greatest examples of what Ullman has called "amenities as a factor in regional growth." A large proportion of the million people in this "Valley of the Sun" are here because they enjoy (and probably feel healthier in) the climate, the outdoor- automobile-centered way of life, the informal social patterns, the variety of recreation, the wide-open country on every horizon—and enjoy the fact that it is all available at a somewhat lower cost of living than in most metropolitan areas. No doubt many of these people also find satisfaction in an ever-changing new townscape, a feeling that they are at the center of "growth" and "progress" in the most "modern" kind of America. In all of this one can see perhaps another of those recurrent exhibits of the "frontier" and the "West" as a kind of exaggeration—almost a caricature—of common national traits. This migration, like all migrations, is selective; if it would seem that central Arizona would exert the strongest pull upon those who are rather hedonistic, footloose, relatively indifferent to traditional ties of family, work, and place, happy to flee old homelands and unattracted by the more cosmopolitan lures of certain other metropolitan areas, there is no reason to think that it will soon run out of potential migrants—indeed most of the American population would likely qualify.

It is far from a new phenomenon, of course, even in its modern phase, and it is at least broadly appropriate that central Arizona has increasingly come to think of itself as the successor to southern California. If it lacks a long ocean shore, it also lacks many of the problems now peculiarly acute in that more famous region. However, such a pattern of thought should logically lead to a consideration that the congestion, smog, and many other problems endemic in the Californian megalopolis are largely the result of the sheer magnitude of uncontrolled immigration and development and that, unless it takes special measures, central Arizona will eventually become more like southern California than it would wish. Unfortunately anti-smog and other measures required are mostly untried, unperfected, or as yet unacceptable to most Americans— and perhaps most especially to the very kind of American most strongly attracted by the lures of Arizona.

EL PASO, TUCSON, AND THE SOUTHERN BORDERLANDS

Tucson and El Paso are quite different cities which have quite similar—and to some extent the very same—hinterlands. Tucson, with a major emphasis upon electronics, recreation, and retirement in a warm-winter desert setting, has much in common with Phoenix; El Paso with its emphasis upon smelting and refining, transportation, and military installations is a rather harsh contrast—but as Tucson draws its local trade and traffic very largely from the country lying to the east and El Paso to a considerable extent from that lying to the west, both are intimately bound to the broad stretch of arid mountain and bolson country between, with its big mining camps, ranches, agricultural oases, and the tourist and traffic service centers along the modern versions of the old Southern Corridor. It is a country with strikingly different kinds of settlements and several different peoples. Spanish-Americans make up a third or more of the population in most of the districts and, furthermore, both Tucson and El Paso have important direct links with Mexico. However, the two cities are critically different in their locations with respect to Mexico and that, perhaps more than anything else, has fostered the over-all contrasts between them.

For the most fundamental fact about El Paso is that it is not only about half Spanish-American in population but is itself but half of the largest international metropolitan complex along the United States-Mexico border. El Paso and Ciudad Juarez form an urban cluster of three-quarters of a million people cramped between the shoulders of the arid ridge through which the Rio Grande has cut the historic "pass." (Fig. 9-4) Another hundred thousand people live in the narrow oases which extend along the river for about fifty miles to the north (Mesilla Valley) and fifty to the southeast.

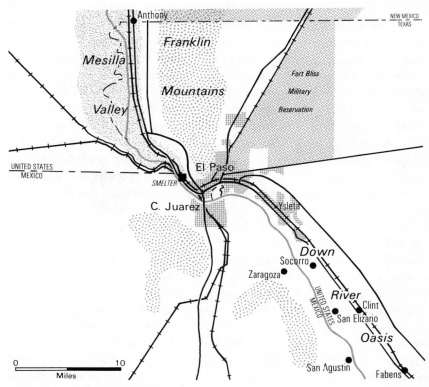

FIG. 9-4. El Paso, Ciudad Juarez

The two national parts of this metropolitan unit are closely articu-
lated and interdependent; the two linguistic cultures live in intimate
association or at least daily awareness of one another. Every day thousands of Mexican workers, shoppers, and those seeking various special
services (such as schools and hospitals) cross the several bridges to El
Paso; and every day thousands of Americans—local residents, sojourners
(such as military personnel), and tourists—cross those same bridges to
the restaurants and bars, night clubs, brothels, bull rings, souvenir
shops, and divorce courts of Ciudad Juarez. Spanish and English newspapers, radio stations, television stations, and cinemas serve the whole
area. Bilingualism is widespread. Nevertheless there are great differences
in the intensity and types of contact between these peoples. At business
and professional levels there is the direct interaction between social
equals among those engaged in international commerce, but a much

larger proportion have no more than rather superficial contacts through intermittent and largely ceremonial affairs, such as exchange visits across the border between service clubs and professional organizations. Aside from those between retailers and customers on both sides of the border, the most widespread contact is that between Anglo employer and Mexican or Mexican-American worker, a close but strongly class-structured relationship. That structure reflects the complete Anglo political, social, and economic dominance over the large but traditionally inert Spanish-speaking proletariat in El Paso. No doubt the existence of a complete and continually expanding Mexican urban society, daily accessible across the river, has considerably retarded acculturation and the participation of this large immigrant population in the life of the American city.

The rapid urban-industrial expansion of El Paso southeast along the railway and highways has encroached heavily upon the narrow downriver oasis. Ysleta, a late seventeenth-century foundation, has been completely engulfed; beyond, Hispano and Anglo settlements are paired, as at San Elizario and Clint: the one near the river, a ramshackle village still focused on a barren church plaza, the other a string of service centers along the busy highway. To the northwest a short barren gap separates the city from the southernmost fields of the Mesilla Valley, but there is a similar duality between the Anglo highway towns (such as Anthony) and the Hispano river villages (such as Chamberino). In both valleys, as in the city, the Anglos completely dominate a large Hispano laboring class.

The omnipresence of Mexico is certainly the most pervasive mark upon El Paso, but there are other prominent symbols of the character of the city and its region. Fort Bliss, wedged deeply into the northeastern corner of the metropolitan area, displays the importance of the military since the beginning of the American settlement. Once a border garrison, it has been transformed into a modern training and research station with a reservation extending far to the north where it joins that of the White Sands Porving Grounds to form a specialized hinterland reaching 150 miles into New Mexico, a long broad stretch of desert useful because of its emptiness, with Alamogordo and Las Cruces serving as scientific and residential outposts on either side.

At the western edge of the city, at the very entrance of the pass, the great stack towering over the blackened copper works is a symbol of El Paso as the focus of a rich mining hinterland. That area is still studded with large productive districts. To the visitor, the vitality of these localities is strikingly apparent in the wholly new residential areas, formed amidst long-ravaged landscapes. Modern suburbs of the old industrial settlement conglomerates, with row upon row of small ranchhouses and ample squares of lawns along broad gently curving streets (e.g. Plantsite and Stargo adjacent to Morenci, Kearney near Hayden); they are bold evidence of sharp improvements in the status of many kinds of industrial labor. Yet the fact that in some of these areas the houses are owned by the mining company and the streets lead to a modern shopping plaza with a single big new company store is also evidence of the continuing paternalistic power of the great corporations over such single-industry settlement districts.

Near the very center of El Paso the swath of railroad yards and the curving sweep of the interstate freeways suggest the importance of the city as a commercial center and traffic focus of a broad band of country extending from the Big Bend of Texas into eastern Arizona. It is a land so limited in water beyond the Rio Grande as to support only very sporadic settlement, with most of its people clustered in little oases, and most of these spaced forty or fifty miles apart along the main highways, each drawing its main sustenance from the passing traffic. Many of these seem little more than garish neon strips. Deming, on the broad flat plain west of the jagged remnants of the Florida Mountains, is considerably more than that. Founded, like many in the region, as a railroad station where well water was available, the extensive underground supply from the Mimbres drainage was eventually tapped to support an agricultural district extending a dozen miles to the south. Nevertheless, its position as an oasis on the southernmost trunk line of the nation has been the chief determinant of its character, and the list of churches in the local telephone book suggests something of what this has meant:

> Iglesia Apostolica de la Fe en Christo Jesus, Inc.
> Assembly of God
> Spanish Assembly of God
> Baptist (two congregations)
> Southern Baptist
> Mexican Baptist
> Christian
> Christian Science
> Church of Christ (two)
> Church of God of Prophecy

Church of Jesus Christ of Latter-Day Saints ("Mormon")
Episcopal
Jehovah's Witnesses
Lutheran
Methodist
Spanish Methodist
Nazarene
Spanish Nazarene
Pentecostal
Presbyterian
Seventh-Day Adventist
Roman Catholic

It is an interesting variety for a town of 7000 and its suggests a relatively fluid and fragmented community, formed by the deposits of migration streams from many parts of America.

Away from that main corridor, each of the many small settlement districts has more likely been formed mainly by only one or two of those streams, as in the Mormon irrigation colonies along the upper Gila and the San Pedro, the Texan-developed cotton areas, the desert retirement colonies; even the mining districts, notoriously heterogeneous as a type, have become more and more Mexican-American in population and therefore Roman Catholic in church membership.

Tucson is the great oasis at the western end of this general area. (Fig. 9-5) Beyond this point the southern trunk line curves northwestward to the central Arizona complex; directly west of Tucson lies the huge desert block of the Papago Indian reservation. To the south the Mexican border is 65 miles away and therein lies the great contrast with El Paso, despite some parallels in history and function. Here the cities of Nogales form a bi-national urban area with 50,000 people and one which serves the specialized border functions. This means that Tucson is not only detached from its Mexican counterpart—its "Juarez"—but also from the main part of that important group of thoroughly bilingual Anglos directly engaged in international and intercultural affairs. There is a considerable traffic of Sonorans coming north to shop in Tucson, but for such persons it is an occasional rather than a daily trip. Thus, whereas Tucson does serve as a travel gateway, some of its firms do much business with Mexico, and its publicists give great stress to the Spanish heritage of the Santa Cruz, the intensity of its bicultural relations is much less than that of El Paso.

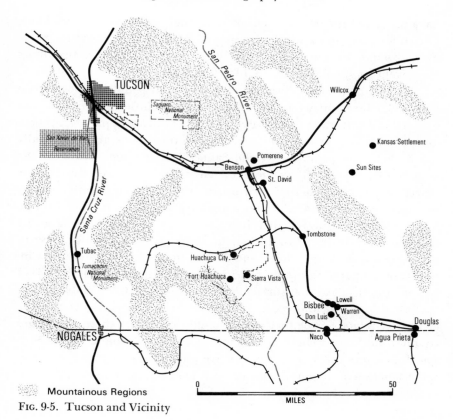

Mountainous Regions

FIG. 9-5. Tucson and Vicinity

Furthermore, it has no large heavy industries; there are important copper mines to the south and to the north but none of the processing plants is in Tucson. It is a railroad division point but a considerably lesser transportation center than El Paso or Phoenix. Such features combined with its location away from the border help to explain why, today, no more than one person in six in this metropolitan area is of Mexican ancestry and the proportion is lessening with the continual heavy influx of Anglos. The several thousand Papago Indians and the smaller community of Yaquis help to perserve some further cultural variety and to maintain links to the country to the west and to the south.

Like Fort Bliss, Davis-Monthan Air Force Base impinges on a corner of the urban area, and the military research activities at Fort Huachuca, the old border counterpart of Fort Bliss seventy miles to the southeast, have prompted the development of whole new towns (e.g. Sierra Vista, Huachuca City) and a wide scattering of small housing tracts for many miles around. In Tucson itself the large one-story modern electronics plant is the most telling industrial landscape symbol.

But by far the most pervasive impression is of people seeking recreation and relaxed living in a desert setting. Facilities for tourists and seasonal residents catering to every price and taste are apparent throughout the metropolitan area, and new housing tracts are spreading rapidly north upon the pediment of the Santa Catalinas and east into the saguaro cactus forest. These new residential areas are not only obvious reflections of the newness of such urban growth and the relative wealth of a considerable segment of the community, they also indicate a subtle but significant cultural change indigenous to the region. For here the national style of the house facing the street over an open expanse of green lawn is no longer dominant. More commonly the house faces inward upon a patio, the yard is enclosed fully or in large part by a wall and its gravel or earthen surface is planted with native shrubs. It is a combination of Anglo, Mexican, and desert elements which creates the distinctive regional style that can be found through much of this border country, but it is nowhere as common or as fully elaborated as in Tucson. It is a product of a very distinctive physical environment, cultural contact, selective migration, wealth and leisure, and interest in a particular style of life.

NORTHERN CORRIDOR AND NAVAHOLANDS

The great thoroughfare across the high plateau west of Albuquerque —now a superhighway as well as a mainline railway—still forms a strong axis for this northern part of the Southwest. (Fig. 9-6) There have been some important modifications in geographical patterns during the past half-century or so, but more significant, some of the common earlier expectations have been utterly confounded. For those great blocks of Indian lands which were then regarded as vast bleak wastelands, as little more than incipient cemeteries for a dying race, are now, quite the contrary, the home of vigorous peoples who seem certain to play an increasingly important role in the region.

Geographical expressions of this remarkable change are numerous, but perhaps best displayed in the Gallup area, an old focus of Indian-white contacts. Gallup, as the main trade center, has long been the

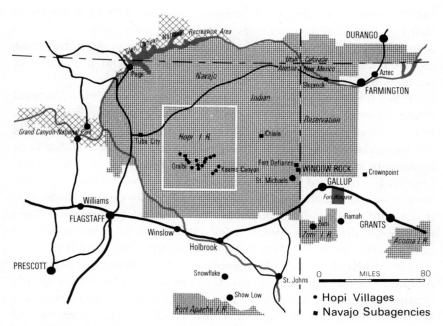

FIG. 9-6. Northern Corridor and Navaholands

principal point for a wide range of Navaho-Anglo contacts, while nearby Fort Defiance and St. Michaels represented special types of inter-cultural relations imposed directly within the Reservation. The first was long a military post and subsequently for a long time, the local headquarters of the Indian Bureau; the second was a major Christian mission. Today a new center near by, Window Rock, represents the fundamental change which has taken place.

Window Rock is new in design, in function, and is a symbol of a rejuvenated culture. It is the capital of the Navaho nation, the political headquarters of what is now virtually a self-governing state-within-the-states. For although the Indian Bureau still holds a veto power, the Navaho Tribal Council, composed of delegates elected from local districts within the Reservation, is the principal decision-making body, and the tribe maintains its own police force and law courts. The Tribal Council Chambers building and Window Rock itself are physical displays of the remarkable power of Navaho culture at once to change and to preserve. The Chambers is a large hogan of stone and timbers in a strikingly modern style; Window Rock, like many smaller places on the Reservation—trading posts, missions, schools—is more a cluster of facilities—administrative agencies, newspaper, radio station—serving a non-resident population than a town in the common American sense of that term. It is a "central place" without the usual proportion of population.

This strong resurgence of the Navaho can be seen as simply the most recent phase of a cultural adaptability demonstrated centuries before in response to contacts with Pueblo peoples and later with the Spanish, but its special power today is closely related to the rather sudden large increments to tribal income derived from mineral leases. The Tribal Council has allocated such windfall wealth to a wide array of public services—schools, sanitation, health care, community centers, roads, electricity—and to a careful selection of local industrial enterprises. Thus the new tribally owned sawmill a few miles north of Window Rock is one of several proud exhibits of Navaho initiative and capabilities.

The results of such developments upon Anglo-Navaho relations are complex. On the one hand certain kinds of contacts have been greatly expanded because of a much greater traffic across the Reservation and because of industrial developments in and adjacent to it; yet on the other hand improvements in facilities and services and the creation of local economic opportunities have begun to stem somewhat the forced exodus of labor. Most important, such developments have begun to release these people from abject poverty and primitiveness and thereby foster a greater pride and dignity in being Navaho. In this way modern technology has had a paradoxical impact: its very adoption represents an important degree of convergence toward the dominant American culture, yet its fruits have helped to sustain a basic divergence, for the Navahos are now discovering that they can compete within American society without having to conform fully to it.

Despite such greatly improved prospects of the Navaho, which are also manifest in somewhat different ways and degrees in the Western Pueblo culture of the nearby Hopi and Zuñi, local Anglo-Indian relationships are still far from harmonious and benign in every respect. Evidence of the heavy human cost of forced culture contacts is still readily apparent in any of the bordering towns: high rates of minor social disorders—drunkenness, brawling, petty thievery; a vagrant population of derelicts adrift between two cultures; discrimination against and exploitation of the Indians in residence, commerce, education, and work.

While the Gallup-Window Rock area is the most important focus of Anglo-Navaho relations, recent economic developments have magnified the importance of Farmington and Flagstaff as other centers of such interaction. Oil and gas and uranium operations have transformed Farmington from a rather isolated trade center into a booming small city. Inevitably the older proportions in the cultural mosaic along the San Juan have been markedly altered. Navahos have been drawn in as laborers and, less successfully, as irrigation farmers, while the Hispanos, who never had more than a foothold, are less significant than before. The character of the community has been shaped primarily by the Mormons and Texans, the former expanding from their little irrigation villages to become prominent in business and the professions, the latter brought in directly or indirectly by the new industries. Together they have a somewhat ambivalent influence: the one an unusually cohesive, socially organized, community-minded group, the other a much more heterogeneous and mobile body of individuals. A narrow-gauge railroad still links Farmington to Alamosa with connections to Pueblo and Denver, but it is an anachronism, and highways and airlines now firmly bind this corner of New Mexico to Albuquerque, while the oil and gas industries sustain important ties with Texas.

Flagstaff, near the opposite corner of the Navaho Reservation, is now more clearly the dominant center of northern Arizona and an increasingly cosmopolitan community. New highways have made it much more of a crossroads and the scenic and recreational attractions of the canyonlands, Navaho country, and San Francisco mountains have drawn ever greater numbers of tourists and sportsmen. The local teachers' college has been transformed and expanded into a university. Navahos, Hopis, Hispanos, Negroes, and Anglos from many areas have come in. Here too the largest source region has been Texas and Oklahoma rather than the Middle West as in the railroad era. Prescott, now off the main road and railroad, its mining hinterland much depleted, nevertheless continues to thrive upon the recreation and retirement amenities of its high basin.

In the Little Colorado country, high on the Mogollon Rim, south of the main corridor, new activities have also lured new people. The forest industries have drawn migrants principally from Texas and the South but also a considerable number from the lumber areas of the Pacific Northwest. The result is a greater variety of communities: Mormon irrigation villages, old Mormon towns now doubled in size and divided in society by the influx of non-Mormon mill workers; company-

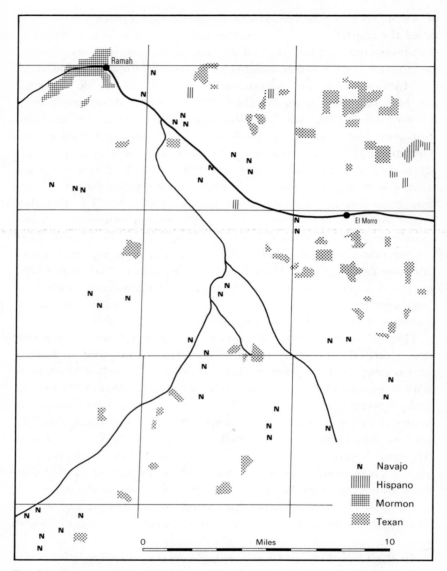

FIG. 9-7. Ramah and Vicinity

owned mill towns; and, just over the Rim to the south, the Apache
tribal sawmill town of Whiteriver. At the very easternmost reaches of
the Little Colorado in New Mexico is the Mormon village of Ramah,
in an area so culturally diverse as to have served as a "laboratory" for

the "Comparative Study of Values in Five Cultures," a famous social science research project. The five cultures are the Mormon, Pueblo (Zuñi), Navaho, Hispano, and Texan. The first two are concentrated in their compact villages and irrigation areas, the others are scattered and to a very considerable extent intermingled over the semi-arid countryside. (Fig. 9-7) (The very distinctive "way of life" of each of these groups, their attitudes toward each of the other peoples, and the latent social tensions among them are amply demonstrated in the long list of publications emanating from this project. Although the area was selected primarily as a rigorous proving ground for certain concepts and methods in social science, the results of the project implicitly underscore the special significance of social geography to any regional analysis of the Southwest.)

Even by Southwestern standards this whole area remains relatively thinly populated and its largest cities are far smaller than those in other subregions. Yet it is growing and changing, and by far the most significant feature is the fact that Anglo-Indian culture contact, which was long so largely a corrosive disintegrative influence of the conquerors upon the conquered, has now clearly evolved to a stage of creative tension between vital societies.

These four subregions together form the Southwest as it has been defined for the purposes of this study: that realm within the United States of Indian, Hispano, and Anglo peoples lying between Texas and California and south of the main body of Mormonland and Colorado. A narrower definition than most, a region even smaller than the two-state area of New Mexico and Arizona, yet one that seems logically to emerge from a review of historical geography.

10 PERSPECTIVES ON REGIONAL

AND CULTURAL RELATIONS

A review of the successive and the cumulative patterns of spatial structure and circulation and of social geography both within the Southwest and in the broader context of the region and its neighbors provides the basis for certain general conclusions and interpretations.

REGIONAL RELATIONS

During the entire Spanish era this Southwest was linked to the outer world by parallel but entirely separate and unconnected longitudinal trails, the one along the Pacific coast to the upper Santa Cruz, the other on the central plateau to the upper Rio Grande. As Tucson was never more than a frontier outpost with no productive hinterland, the first was of little significance, but the second would form part of the enduring spatial structure of the region. In the Mexican period the opening of the wagon road to Missouri and the pack trail to California changed New Mexico from a remote terminus to a position on trafficways of continental dimensions, even if as yet of little continental importance. These broad relationships were redirected and magnified with unusual immediacy and power at the outset of the American period because the Mexican cession included California as well as New Mexico and because of the great Gold Rush to the Sierra Nevada. Had New Mexico alone been taken at that time with no radical discoveries of new wealth, the Missouri connection would have gained firm ascendancy over that of Chihuahua, but it would have led to a relatively insignificant province in a remote corner of the nation.

As it happened, New Mexico suddenly found itself astride a pair of new latitudinal trafficways, and its own development would be inexorably bound ever after, in some considerable degree, with these national trunk lines to California. The northernmost of this pair of routes crossed the old longitudinal axis at Albuquerque; the southern crossed at the El Paso oasis and led on west to tap the very end of the Spanish Pacific axis at Tucson, making the first lateral link between these two. Thus three sides of the basic grid were formed in the first years of American rule; the fourth, the longitudinal connection in Arizona, was delayed by the difficulties of the terrain and the slowness of economic development. Established in the era of military wagon roads and subsequently reinforced through railway, highway, and freeway eras, this grid has formed a relatively stable spatial structure for the Southwest for more than a century.

To state this is in effect to describe the Southwest as a group of parts rather than a functional whole, for a grid is a set of intersections and has no focus. The sequential emergence of those parts and their changing proportionate importance is a major feature of the historical geography of the Southwest. (Fig. 10-1)

During the Spanish and Mexican eras there was a clear focus, but only because so much of the region lay beyond control. Spanish New Mexico began as an unusually isolated and self-contained nucleus and it developed into a clear example of an autonomous "provincial system": an extensive region bound together over a meager network of cart roads and pack trails, with a few small trade centers and a single administrative capital; largely self-sustaining, it was connected to the main body of its nation and to the larger world of commerce only by intermittent—usually no more than annual—movements over a single long road across the wilderness. During the Mexican period the region was somewhat enlarged but it remained no less separate, though it gained new connections across its girdling wastelands to other commercial networks.

That same discrete provincial system was continually enlarged under the Americans, refocused upon Albuquerque, the main intersection on the emergent grid, but it could not be so extended as to encompass the whole of this Southwest. Distance, intervening desolation, specialized functions, and parallel competitive trafficways allowed other centers to emerge at analogous points within the grid. Thus El Paso, with its peculiar border role and captive mining hinterland, developed concur-

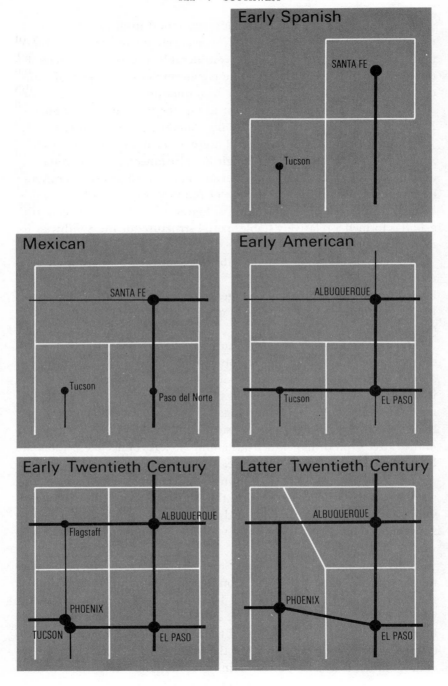

Fig. 10-1. Sequential Regional Structure

rently to dominate the southeastern area. At the northwest intersection, the relative meagerness of the economic base has always been reflected in the relatively small size and more limited functions of Flagstaff. In the southwestern section, the situation has been unusually dynamic, with Tucson, the historic focus, overtaken and increasingly overwhelmed by Phoenix.

Indeed the power of Phoenix is so great as to place the western half of the Southwest increasingly under its dominance. A true metropolis, it subordinates Flagstaff as well as Tucson. Since it does so, it becomes increasingly necessary to see the basic spatial structure of the Southwest as a triangular articulation of metropolitan fields—Phoenix, Albuquerque, and El Paso—rather than as a rectangular set of trafficways connecting four analogous regional centers. To the degree that these three are discrete fields, we may regard the Southwest as now having three "provincial systems" rather than one. But in fact they are not sharply separate from one another and together they are not so detached from larger systems as the term might suggest, for the Southwest is clearly enmeshed within a national network. Nevertheless, despite ever closer integration and the radical spatial character of air traffic, interregional connections still vary a good deal in pattern and significance.

Despite the multiplication of routes, large sectors of the once encompassing wilderness remain in some degree unaffected. The broad Mohave Desert still distinctly separates the southern California metropolitan complex from that of central Arizona. Yet developments spaced along the Colorado River, which bisects the desert, continue to modify the nature and severity of this separation. The reservoirs created by the series of dams sustain several agricultural oases and have become increasingly important recreational attractions. However, by far the most imposing development is Lake Havasu City, founded in 1964, promoted nation-wide by a major industrial corporation, and comprehensively planned to become a diversified community of 60,000 persons. Located near the state border, halfway between Phoenix and Los Angeles, such a place may well become the main unit of a considerably larger "dispersed city"—a set of centers complementary rather than hierarchical in their relationships, which together perform the functions of a city much larger than any one. Should it equal the hopes of its planners it would significantly reduce the degree of separation between the Arizona and southern California systems.

That particular scheme is only one of the more striking examples of the modern capability of creating very comfortable living environments in the midst of the tropical desert and of the high attractive power of such centers within the relatively dynamic American settlement system. A great precedent for such transforming developments lies just 150 miles to the north within the tip of Nevada, where Las Vegas was changed from a small routeway oasis into an internationally famous entertainment and convention center. To be sure the special qualities of Las Vegas have been critically dependent upon the special political environment of Nevada, and thus the explosive emergence of this vibrant center is critically related to the political partitioning of this Southwestern desert area. Las Vegas has had marked effect upon interregional and national traffic patterns, and is a major point where the Arizona and California systems interlock, eccentric to their direct border zone.

Las Vegas is also a pivotal point on one of the three routeways connecting the main body of Mormon settlement with its southerly outliers in the Southwest. Highway 89, crossing the Colorado River by alternate routes just above and just below the old Mormon crossing at Lee's Ferry, is the modern version of an equally old and more direct link. Despite the rapidly growing importance of the new recreational resources of Lake Powell, the complete lack of settlement over broad areas of the plateau, together with the now almost continuous strip of national reserved lands along the Colorado River, would seem likely to sustain the clear separation of the two regions along this border. Any southward filling in from the Mormon region would encounter the sharply defined barrier of the Navaho Reservation.

The third link has been by way of the San Juan country. Farmington has always had a distinctly border position, pivotal to the Mormon, New Mexico, and Colorado settlement and circulatory systems. Now the focus of a more populous and developed area, it remains a somewhat discrete center. In its rather balanced population of Mormons and non-Mormons it represents a more sharply defined contact between Mormondom and the Southwest. Yet, because of the broad desolation of the canyonlands its local Mormon hinterland remains more separated from the main Utah cities than from Albuquerque.

To the northeast the pattern of interregional relations is very different, with a direct interlocking of the Colorado and New Mexico systems. Durango, Alamosa, Walsenburg, and Trinidad are the principal points of connection. Historically, they lie along the zone where the northward expansion of Hispanos was blunted and intersected by the westward Anglo movements from the Colorado piedmont. The early railroad system set the direction of circulation strongly focusing these centers upon Pueblo and Denver and connections to the east rather than south to Santa Fe and Albuquerque. The marked bicultural Anglo and Hispano population in all of these Colorado cities makes them generally similar to many in New Mexico, but they all lie beyond the limits of the old Hispano-dominated countryside. There are Spanish-Americans in every county of Colorado and many of them have ancestral roots in New Mexico, but they are everywhere adjuncts of Anglo activities, recruited, sometimes long ago, as a labor force for farms, ranches, mines, smelters, and railroads. Colorado is therefore an outer sphere into which the Hispanos have moved but which they have never dominated; it has ever been alien ground wherein Hispano-Anglo relationships have been the reverse of the New Mexican sequence. To the extent that these former New Mexicans maintain social ties with kinfolk and ancestral villages in Rio Arriba, they sustain a significant interlocking of distinct social regions.

Southwest and Middle West touch in the northeastern corner of New Mexico, where grain farming was extended from Kansas into what was once Hispano pastoral country. It is a narrow sector of the Southwest's border, historically unstable and without sharp definition in the mosaic of ranching and farming. But its great importance is not as a boundary but as a corridor of major connections. Ever since the Santa Fe Trail the principal links between the Southwest and the core of the nation have funneled through this corner by way of Raton Pass or more directly across the Cimarron country. The non-stop flights from Chicago to Albuquerque, to Tucson, and to Phoenix are but the latest in a sequence of trunk line services along this axis.

The eastern border has been by far the most unstable, and for more than a century every change has meant a contraction of the Southwest or at least a diminution of the hold of its people along that side. The cattlemen spreading up the Pecos Valley and across the Llano Estacado obliterated the broad desolate buffer and ever after New Mexico has lain athwart the main direction of Texan expansion. The solid wave of farmers across the high flatlands impressed the firm hold of Texans upon the southeastern corner of New Mexico, a hold subsequently reinforced by the oil industry. Less massive movements of people and capital have penetrated deeply into the state. The Pecos Valley is strongly Texan in population and orientation, the high insular Capitan and

Sacramento mountains to the west have become an important Texan playground, and the main towns and cities along the Rio Grande and on the trafficways farther west have all felt some considerable impact. Thus in social geography, the interregional relationship is one of gradations of Texan influence, decreasing in intensity and areal comprehensiveness westward. In terms of circulation systems, there is no sharp separation of metropolitan fields. Roswell occupies a border position between Albuquerque and the much more complex Texan system. Clovis and Hobbs are clearly part of that system, directly subordinate to Amarillo, Lubbock, and Midland-Odessa. On the far southeast, the Texan Trans-Pecos remains a thinly occupied country crossed by major trafficways which bring it into focus on El Paso.

The international boundary is so decisive in its importance to so wide a range of interregional relations as to be accepted as a precise southern edge to the Southwest, despite the fact that with refernce to some features it cuts across a broad cultural borderland. Interregional relations are in fact almost entirely focused upon the two points at El Paso-Juarez and Nogales. The latter is clearly less important for it is wholly a creation of the geometrical boundary line, while the former is an important oasis, industrial center, and route junction as well. For more than a century El Paso-Juarez, especially, has been a major funnel for the influences of each country upon the other. American money, goods, and ideas have radiated over a broad area and helped to stamp the "North" as a distinctive region within Mexico. The principal flow in return has been people, out of that North into the American Southwest. Although restricted in their economic position and social participation, these Mexican-Americans have even more clearly stamped the southern borderlands of this Southwest as a distinctive subregion and they sustain strong bonds of connection across the international boundary.

In summary, the Southwest has direct interregional relations with California, Mormonland, Colorado, the Middle West, Texas, and Mexico. (Fig. 10-2) Of these, Texas impinges most heavily and aggressively. Texas, Mexico, and the Middle West are the main sources of immigrants. For a long time California was significant chiefly as a magnet pulling people through the Southwest, but recently a direct eastward influence has been exerted. Indeed, the Southwest appears to be increasingly squeezed between Texas and California, two of the most distinctive and dynamic regions in America. Nevertheless, though each has

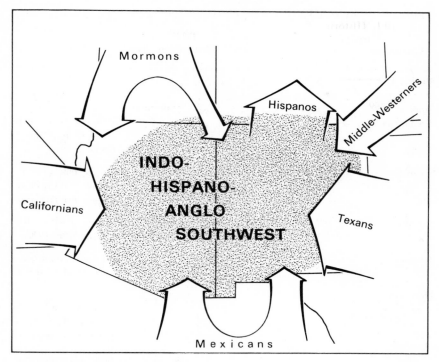

FIG. 10-2. Border Encroachments

much greater demographic, economic, and in some ways cultural power, the Southwest is not really in imminent danger of being captured and overrun, divided between and submerged beneath these two. Distance, desolation, and its own distinctive character still markedly differentiate it from its neighbors.

CULTURAL RELATIONS

When first explored by the Spanish the Southwest was an area of several distinct peoples, and it has become ever more complex during the four centuries following. Several of the aboriginal groups persisted and new indigenous cultures gradually arose from sustained intercultural contact. Subsequent to that initial long tenuous implantation of European people into the upper Rio Grande, the region has lain in the path of a whole sequence of important migrations: the general westward movement of the American continental conquest, the special aggressive

TABLE 10-1. Historical Pattern of Peoples in the Southwest

Group	Time 1600	1800	1900	1970	Provenience	Comment
Pueblo	x	x	x	x		
Pima-Papago	x	x	x	x		
Apache	x	x	x	x	Aboriginal	
Comanche	x	x				Remnant removed to reservation in Oklahoma
Spanish	x	x			Immigrant	Largely officials and priests; withdraws or merges into Hispano
Navaho		x	x	x	Local Indigenous	Emerges from acculturation after 1600
Hispano		x	x	x		Emerges from miscegenation after 1600
Northern Anglo-American			x	x		Commerce and ranching; includes early Jewish merchants
Mormon			x	x		
Texan			x	x		Also Oklahomans
Mexican-American			x	x	Immigrant	
General Anglo-American				x		From all parts of U. S.; irrigation, recreational, and urban centers
Afro-American				x		

x = Significantly Present

thrusts from Texas, the northward infiltration of Mexicans attracted by an expanding American economy, the marked southward bias of Brigham Young's vision of a Mormon commonwealth, and the strong attractions of warmer climates and western landscapes upon Americans in the latter twentieth century. The cumulative result is nearly a dozen recognizably distinct peoples in the area today. (Table 10-1)

While the Southwest has been involved in the tensions of a plural society ever since the conquering Spanish settled alongside the Pueblo

Indians, the degree and character of pluralism are of course dependent upon the scale of generalization. No broad area within the Southwest ever contained at any time in this sequence this entire list of groups, and, as indicated in previous chapters, the major subregions have always differed considerably as to particular peoples and proportions. Such differences are related to aboriginal territorial patterns, the geographical selectivity of the various migrations (whether intruding directly upon previous peoples or seeking more or less vacant ground), and subsequent internal movements (as where aboriginal peoples have been lured out of their mono-cultural reservation enclaves into adjacent heterogeneous centers).

Viewed broadly and focusing upon relations between groups of greatest contrast, three major regions or zones of cultural contact seem most apparent within the Southwest: (1) northern New Mexico, with Pueblo, Hispano, and various Anglo groups; (2) the southern borderlands, with Mexican-Americans and Anglos in close contact, especially in the border cities and mining districts; (3) the Northern Corridor, wherein every town is a point of intense Indian-Anglo contact. Much less obvious because of less cultural distinction among the several Anglo groups are the westward gradations of Texan influence, and the more geographically selective Mormon pattern. (Fig. 10-3) Wherever they settle in considerable number, Texans are a recognizable group even if

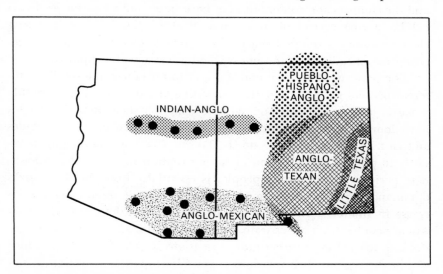

FIG. 10-3. Interregional Areas of Culture Contact

not a highly self-conscious one. Mormons are an unusually cohesive people and although they dominate no more than local districts they do represent an important cultural component in much of the western half of the Southwest.

The tensions inherent in plural societies tend to vary indirectly with this scale of areal generalization: most intense at the level of daily contact in the local community, lessening through the looser associations of larger districts and regions. Because such tension is often most overt in the realm of politics, the hierarchy of political territories is an important framework within which to view such matters. Where two or more of these groups share a single school district or an incorporated town or city, the tensions are likely to be the greatest. Dual communities and city-suburban complexes are other special political territorial situations of high potential conflict. Although the county is a larger and less intimate association of peoples, its governmental power over various public services, the administration of justice, and patronage make it an important areal context for the expression of social issues. Finally, the state provides the largest subnational political arena for the play of such competitive forces. Further complicating this political hierarchy are the various special federally administered areas, especially Indian and military reservations. The Southwest is replete with examples of such situations. New Mexico is the very archetype at the state-wide level, and the counties and communities of both states and westernmost Texas exhibit a rich variety of socio-geopolitical relationships, some rather clear and simple, others remarkably complex; some seemingly benign, others chronically tense and uneasy, and a few actually explosive.

The patterns of relative political and social power among these different peoples within any particular setting are, of course, never simply a matter of proportionate populations. Whatever their numbers, Anglos have dominated every major district of the Southwest for many decades and clearly will continue to do so. To say this, however, is not necessarily to suggest either a kind of static situation in which the subordinate position of non-Anglo peoples is essentially fixed, or that Anglo dominance will increase commensurate with their almost certain increase in numbers. In fact, there are many indications that the non-Anglo peoples, both as separate groups and in broader associations, are working toward some rather radical revisions in relative social positions within the region. Such revisions depend less upon an assertion of numerical strength (although in many counties and communities there is still the possibility of applying the political power of their numbers to a much greater extent) than upon a vigorous overt insistence that Anglos recognize and accept the integrity and equality of non-Anglo peoples as distinct cultures within a genuinely pluralistic American society.

The basic internal strength of these local cultures has long been displayed in the simple fact of their persistence in the face of powerful pressures for assimilation into dominant national patterns. What is new in the Southwest among these groups is a change in attitudes about the nature and possibilities of their position, a change from seeing themselves as a besieged remnant desperately hanging on to the hard core of their culture, to a feeling of pride in seeing themselves as creative and expansive peoples with something special to contribute to the life of America. It is, of course, a very difficult transition, critically dependent upon the quality of local leadership and upon the particular internal culture patterns, special history, and geographic context of each group. Some are clearly much farther along than others, with the Navahos as probably the most notable evidence of the latent power which can be released.

It is somewhat paradoxical, perhaps, that the Indians, though complete captives and wards of the federal government, are in a better position to make this transition than the Spanish-Americans. Their advantage lies partly in that the reservation provides a more or less unified territorial base and partly in that the policies of the federal government are set by administrative rule rather than simple local political power and thus are more open to rational change. The paternal hand of the United States has always been heavy, but the basic policies of the Bureau of Indian Affairs have been redefined several times over the past century, each change representing a different view of the appropriate position for Indians as a people within the United States. It is now clear that the Indians are ready to insist that they themselves be allowed to define that position, to have the dominant role in determining such federal policies. Such a change is surely a major step toward a more equitable pluralism.

The Hispanos of northern New Mexico were no less captives of the American state than the aborigines, but as a Christian and Spanish-speaking people were logically accepted as "civilized" and given citizenship instead of becoming wards of the federal government. Their specific "cultural rights" as regards language and religion were ostensibly protected by treaty, federal law, and the constitution of the State of New

Mexico. But in fact their protection was dependent upon local political power and a sympathetic understanding of their position as a non-Anglo minority. From the first they were forced to adapt to Anglo concepts of law and thus to compete at a serious disadvantage. In regard to concepts of property it was a crippling disadvantage, and as Anglo numbers and vested interests became ever more powerful, Hispano control of their own destinies in their own homeland dwindled. Extrication from more than a century of that disastrous trend has proven extremely difficult and is yet in an early and unpredictable phase. The 1967 eruption under a charismatic leader, of the "nativist" *Alianza Federal de los Pueblos Libres* movement (translated by that group as "Federal Alliance of Free City-States"), was a telling measure of the smoldering desperation felt by many Hispanos. The basic program of that movement calls for restoration of old land grants to Hispano control. As this would seem to face almost insuperable political and legal obstacles, it is easy to dismiss it as unrealistic. Anglos commonly insist that the only feasible solution is to draw the Hispanos out of their poverty pockets in the mountains of New Mexico to new jobs and lives elsewhere within the mainstream of American life. But that "solution" has been in operation, in effect if not as a program, for many decades, as attested by the forced exodus of Hispano laborers, and it is surely significant that this first truly indigenous radical political movement stresses just the opposite. The basic importance of land and community, the right to remain in their homeland, is a tenet of all the many Hispano groups and spokesmen. As always in New Mexico, there are many Anglos who sympathize, and numerous programs have been proposed to revitalize Hispano village culture. But the fact that His-panos are now beginning to speak more positively and act more directly to shape their own future is the main reason to be confident that they will have an enduring and creative place in American life despite the really formidable difficulties they will face for many years to come.

The peculiar history and location of the northern New Mexican His-panos have always made them a very distinctive group within the whole body of Spanish-Americans in the United States. Their political pro-grams express their very particular situation but inevitably they will ally themselves increasingly with broader movements affecting their cul-tural kin. Recent efforts to politicize the Mexican-American population in El Paso are the main local evidence in the Southwest of fundamental developments underway to redress the chronic discrepancy between numbers and power in the relationships of Anglos and Mexican-Americans. The geography of this movement reaches from the San Joaquin Valley of California into south Texas and north over Colorado. So far, the major areas of active change (and therefore high tension) are in the agricultural labor districts of California and Texas and in such urban centers as Denver and San Antonio, but the impact of such actions inevitably will ramify through the smaller cities, mining towns, farms and ranches of the whole Southwest, bringing a new turbulence to local politics as an initial aspect in the long difficult redefinition of roles to be played in this bicultural borderland.

When viewed in broader context it seems apparent that the strong surge of such movements in the 1960's has been directly influenced by the far more powerful upwellings from America's largest minority, the Afro-Americans. In the Southwest, Negroes constitute a relatively small and new group and are heavily concentrated in a few areas, such as Phoenix and some of the Arizona agricultural laborer towns. Tensions arising directly from their presence will therefore be very localized. But the nation-wide assertion of "Black Power" in opposition to the traditional caste-like discrimination imposed by "White America" has clearly had an electrifying effect upon other non-white minorities. "Red Power" and "Brown Power" are now analogous concepts and slogans as Indians and mestizo Spanish-Americans, respectively, each begin to develop a sense of unity encompassing their many discrete groups (the Spanish-Americans more commonly use "La Raza" as a collective term). In this way, national and regional movements seeking a redefinition of America as a plural society become increasingly interdependent.

Thus the Southwest now looms as an area particularly critical to the changing patterns of American society. Heretofore two other broad regions have been central to this national process. The most famous has been the Northeast, that urban-industrial crucible of the notorious "melting pot" into which all the national and religious varieties of Europe poured during a century of mass immigration. Only in the last generation has it become quite evident that the product of that process has not been, nor is soon likely to be, the uniform "American" alloy so commonly expected. Instead there has emerged a much modified but still complexly variegated population in which ethnic differences still impinge upon a wide range of social issues and can still be the source of considerable social tension. The growing realization not only that this is the case, but that such variety can be the source of great cultural enrichment, is what has given rise to the concept of pluralism as a fresh

American ideal. The South is equally famous as a special social area, but its two peoples were so long locked in a caste-like structure that the concept of pluralism was applicable in no more than the most limited sense. However, the revolt of the Negroes against such pervasive discrimination has rather suddenly made Black-White relations the most critical test of the concept in any larger sense. Although because of twentieth-century migrations, the North and the West are faced with that particular test as well, the South, with its special history and geography (especially with its Black rural as well as urban population), remains the most significant area. As Indians and Spanish-Americans join in this revolution, the whole southwestern part of the nation becomes a third area peculiarly important to this powerful process. Such an area is so broad and internally varied as to constitute a single region only with reference to such general social movements. Within that gross frame lies the Southwest as herein defined, an area which also lacks any central focus, uniformity of pattern, or strong self-consciousness, yet an area sufficiently interconnected in its parts and separated from bordering areas to warrant recognition as a distinctive region within the nation. It is a distinction which arises from the special historical geography of its dozen peoples and it is thereby a distinction which is likely to become much more significant and apparent as America moves painfully forward in its redefinition of the national society.

BIBLIOGRAPHY

The following list of sources may seem disproportionately long for so short a book but it arises from the special character of the work. Because there have been almost no studies on the historical social geography of the region the areal patterns of the several peoples have had to be pieced together from a great variety of very local or otherwise rather specialized studies. Although some of the items listed are somewhat tangential in their main theme to those of this book, I nevertheless wish to acknowledge my dependence upon them.

Because of the varied character of the items, I have sought to serve the general reader by separating those studies which deal with the whole Southwest, a state, or some other rather broad part of the area or history, from those which are narrower and localized.

Sources used extensively but not listed include various volumes of the United States Census (including the special volumes on churches or religious bodies—especially 1906 and 1926—and on the Spanish Surname Population, 1960); *Arizona Highways* and *New Mexico Magazine,* published monthly by the respective states; a wide variety of published maps; and current newspaper reports, especially from *The New York Times.* I wish also to call attention to a very important work published too late to be used: Nancie L. González, *The Spanish-Americans of New Mexico,* Albuquerque: University of New Mexico Press, 1969.

Finally, as any such list as follows is deceptive as to degree of dependence, I wish to acknowledge a special indebtedness to and admiration for a few really major works: those of Spicer, Horgan, Lamar, Vogt, and Beck.

General

Allen, James B., *The Company Town in the American West,* Norman: University of Oklahoma Press, 1966.

Arizona, A State Guide, American Guide Series, New York: Hastings House, 1940.

Arizona Statistical Review, Phoenix: Valley National Bank, annual (various issues).

The Arizona Story, Phoenix: Arizona Development Board, 1966.

Bailey, Wilfrid C., "A Typology of Arizona Communities," *Economic Geography,* 26 (April 1950), 94-104.

Baker, Simon and Thomas J. McCleneghan, *An Arizona Economic and Historic Atlas,* Tucson: College of Business and Public Administration, University of Arizona, 1966.

Bancroft, Hubert Howe, *History of the North Mexican States and Texas,* Vol. I, 1531–1800, San Francisco: A. O. Bancroft & Co., 1884.

Barnes, Elinor J., "Arizona's People Since 1910," *Arizona Review of Business and Public Administration,* 13 (January 1964), 3-10.

Barnes, Elinor J., "Tracing Arizona Migration," *Arizona Review of Business and Public Administration,* 13 (November 1964), 6-9.

Beck, Warren A. and Ynez D. Haase, *Historical Atlas of New Mexico,* Norman: University of Oklahoma Press, 1969.

Beck, Warren A., *New Mexico, A History of Four Centuries,* Norman: University of Oklahoma Press, 1962.

Berger, William M., *Berger's Tourists' Guide to New Mexico,* Kansas City, Mo.: Ramsey, Millett & Hudson, 1883.

Brand, Donald D., "The Early History of the Range Cattle Industry in Northern Mexico," *Agricultural History,* 35 (October 1961), 132-39.

Bufkin, Donald, "The Lost County of Pah-Ute," *Arizoniana,* 5 (Summer 1964), 1-11.

Calvin, Ross, *Sky Determines, An Interpretation of the Southwest,* Albuquerque: University of New Mexico Press, revised ed., 1965.

Carroll, Ray L., "Gross, Blackwell & Company, Mercantile Capitalists in the Southwest 1867–1902," unpub. M.A. thesis (bus. adm.), University of New Mexico, 1965.

Chambers, R. L., "New Mexico: Land of Disenchantment," *Frontier,* 1 (January 1, 1950), 4-6.

Christian, Jane M., "The Navajo, A People in Transition," *Southwestern Studies,* 2 (Part 1, Fall 1964, 1-35 and Part 2, Winter 1964, 39-69).

C(onway), A. W., "Village Types in the Southwest," *Landscape,* 2 (Spring 1952), 14-19.

Cross, Jack L., Elizabeth H. Shaw, and Kathleen Scheifele, eds., *Arizona, its People and Resources,* Tucson: University of Arizona Press, 1960.

Culbert, James L., "Distribution of Spanish-American Population in New Mexico," *Economic Geography,* 19 (April 1943), 171-76.

Directory of Churches and Religious Organizations in Arizona, Phoenix: Arizona Statewide Archival and Records Project, March 1940.

Directory of Churches and Religious Organizations in New Mexico, 1940, Albuquerque: The New Mexico Historical Records Survey, 1940.

Donnell, F. S., "The Confederate Territory of Arizona, as Compiled from Official Sources," *New Mexico Historical Review,* 17 (April 1942), 148-63.

Donnelly, Thomas C., "New Mexico: An Area of Conflicting Cultures," in Thomas C. Donnelly, ed., *Rocky Mountain Politics,* Albuquerque: University of New Mexico Press, 1940, 218-51.

Dozier, Edward P., "Rio Grande Pueblos," in Edward H. Spicer, ed., *Perspectives in American Indian Culture Change,* Chicago: University of Chicago Press, 1961, 94-186.

Ewing, Floyd F., Jr., "The Mule as a Factor in the Development of the Southwest," *Arizona and the West,* 5 (Winter 1963), 315-26.

Faulk, Odie B., *Too Far North—Too Far South: The Controversial Boundary Survey and the Epic Story of the Gadsden Purchase,* Los Angeles: Westernlore Press, 1967.

Fergusson, Erna, *New Mexico: A Pageant of Three Peoples,* New York: Alfred A. Knopf, Inc., 1951.

Fierman, Floyd S., "Peddlers and Merchants on the Southwest Frontier 1850–1880," *Password,* 8 (1963).

Forbes, Jack D., *Apache, Navaho and Spaniard,* Norman: University of Oklahoma Press, 1960.

Foster, H. Mannie, "History of Mormon Settlements in Mexico and New Mexico," unpub. M.A. thesis (hist.), University of New Mexico, 1937.

Frost, Max, compiler and ed., *New Mexico, Its Resources, Climate, Geography, Geology, History, Statistics, Present Condition and Future Prospects,* Santa Fe: Bureau of Immigration of the Territory of New Mexico, 1894.

Fuller, Varden and E. D. Tetreau, "Volume and Characteristics of Migration to Arizona 1930–39," *Arizona Agric. Exp. Station Bulletin No. 176* (November 1941).

Greever, William S., *Arid Domain, The Santa Fe Railway and Its Western Land Grant,* Stanford: Stanford University Press, 1954.

Greever, William S., "Railway Development in the Southwest," *New Mexico Historical Review,* 32 (January 1957), 151-203.

Haley, J. Evetts, "The Comanchero Trade," *Southwestern Historical Quarterly,* 38 (January 1935), 157-76.

Hamilton, David, "Imperial Texas and Its Satellite States," *Frontier: The Voice of the New West,* 10 (August 1959), 9-10.

Haskett, Bert, "Early History of the Cattle Industry in Arizona," *Arizona Historical Review,* 6 (October 1935), 3-42.

Haskett, Bert, "History of the Sheep Industry in Arizona," *Arizona Historical Review,* 7 (July 1936), 3-49.

Hewett, Edgar L. and Wayne L. Mawzy, *Landmarks of New Mexico,* Albuquerque: University of New Mexico Press, 3rd ed., 1953.

Holmes, Jack E., *Politics in New Mexico,* Albuquerque: University of New Mexico Press, 1967.

Hook, Ralph C., Jr., and Paul D. Simkins, "Recent Migration to Arizona," *The Bureau of Business Services, Abstract No. 309* (June 1959).

Horgan, Paul, *Great River, The Rio Grande in North American History,* New York and Toronto: Rinehart & Company, Inc., 1954. 2 vols.

Irion, Frederick C., "New Mexico: The Political State" in Frank H. Jonas, ed., *Western Politics,* Salt Lake City: University of Utah Press, 1961, 223-46.

Jackson, J. B., "First Comes The House," *Landscape,* 9 (Winter 1959–60), 26-32.

Johansen, Sigurd, "The Population of New Mexico: Its Composition and Changes," *New Mexico Agric. Exp. Station Bulletin No. 273,* June 1940.

Jones, Billy M., *Health-Seekers in the Southwest, 1817–1900,* Norman: University of Oklahoma Press, 1967.

Jones, Oakah L., Jr., *Pueblo Warriors and Spanish Conquest,* Norman: University of Oklahoma Press, 1966.

Judah, Charles B., *Recruitment of Candidates from the Northern and Eastern Counties to the New Mexico House of Representatives—1956,* Division of Research, Department of Government, University of New Mexico, January 1961.

La Farge, Oliver, "New Mexico" in *American Panorama,* Garden City: Doubleday & Co., Inc., [1947–1960], Part 2, 216-29.

Lamar, Howard Roberts, *The Far Southwest, 1842–1912, A Territorial History,* New Haven and London: Yale University Press, 1966.

Larson, Robert W., "Statehood for New Mexico 1888–1912," unpub. Ph.D. dissertation (hist.), University of New Mexico, 1961.

Lawrence, Eleanor, "Mexican Trade Between Santa Fe and Los Angeles 1830–1848," *California Historical Society Quarterly,* 10 (March 1931), 27-39.

Leaming, George F., "Copper Smelting and Refining: What Will the Nation Need?" *Arizona Review,* 16 (February 1967), 10-16.

Leaming, George F. and John H. Clark, "Where Does Arizona's Copper Go?" *Arizona Review of Business and Public Administration,* 15 (January, 1966), 11-15.

Long, William W., "A History of Mining in New Mexico During the Spanish and Mexican Periods," unpub. M.A. thesis (hist.), University of New Mexico, 1964.

Manuel, Herschel T., *Spanish-Speaking Children of the Southwest, Their Education and Public Welfare,* Austin: University of Texas Press, 1965.

Martin, Douglas D., *An Arizona Chronology, Statehood 1913–1936,* Tucson: University of Arizona Press, 1966.

Masters, Mary J., "New Mexico's Struggle for Statehood, 1903–1907," unpub. M.A. thesis (hist.), University of New Mexico, 1942.

McClintock, J. H., *Mormon Settlement in Arizona,* Phoenix: Manufacturing Stationers, 1921.

McWilliams, Carey, *North from Mexico, The Spanish-speaking People of the United States,* Philadelphia and New York: J. B. Lippincott Co., 1949.

Meaders, Margaret, *The Indian Situation in New Mexico,* Albuquerque: Bureau of Business Research, The University of New Mexico, 1963.

Moorhead, Max L., *New Mexico's Royal Road, Trade and Travel on the Chihuahua Trail,* Norman: University of Oklahoma Press, 1958.

Morgan, Neil, *Westward Tilt, The American West Today,* New York: Random House, 1963.

Morrisey, Richard J., "The Early Range Cattle Industry in Arizona," *Agricultural History,* 24 (July 1950), 151-56.

New Mexico, A Guide to the Colorful State, New York: American Guide Series, Hastings House, 1940.

Nostrand, Richard Lee, "The Hispanic-American Borderland: A Regional, Historical Geography," unpub. Ph.D. dissertation (geog.), University of California, Los Angeles, 1968.

Parish, William J., *The Charles Ilfield Company, A Study of the Rise and Decline of Mercantile Capitalism in New Mexico,* Cambridge: Harvard University Press, 1961.

Parish, William J., "The German Jew and the Commercial Revolution in Territorial New Mexico 1850–1900," *New Mexico Quarterly,* 29 (Autumn, 1959), 307-32.

Pollock, Paul W., *Arizona Centennial Edition,* Phoenix: Paul W. Pollock, 1962.

Ramsey, Dwight M., Jr., "A Statistical Survey of Voting Behavior in New Mexico," unpub. M.A. thesis (govt.), University of New Mexico, 1951.

Rice, Ross E., "Amazing Arizona: Politics in Transition," in Frank H. Jonas, ed., *Western Politics,* Salt Lake City: University of Utah Press, 1961, 41-68.

Russell, John C., "State Regionalism in New Mexico," unpub. Ph.D. dissertation (pol. sci.), Stanford University, 1938.

Sacks, B., "The Creation of the Territory of Arizona," *Arizona and the West,* 5 (Spring and Summer 1963), 29-62, 109-48.

Sanchez, George I., *Forgotten People: A Study of New Mexicans,* Albuquerque: Calvin Horn, 1967.

Scholes, France V., "Civil Government and Society in New Mexico in the Seventeenth Century," *New Mexico Historical Review,* 10 (April 1935), 71-111.

Seligiman, Gustav Leonard, "The El Paso and Northeastern Railroad System and its Economic Influence in New Mexico," unpub. M.A. thesis (hist.), New Mexico State University, 1958.

Shryock, Henry S., Jr., *Population Mobility Within the United States,* Chicago: Community and Family Study Center, University of Chicago, 1964.

Simmons, Marc, "Settlement Patterns and Village Plans in Colonial New Mexico," *Journal of the West,* 8 (January 1968), 7-21.

Spicer, Edward H., *Cycles of Conquest, The Impact of Spain, Mexico, and the United States on the Indians of the Southwest, 1533–1960,* Tucson: University of Arizona Press, 1962.

Sprague, Marshall, *The Mountain States,* New York: Time-Life Books, 1967.

Taylor, James Woodall, "Geographic Bases of the Gadsden Purchase," *Journal of Geography,* 57 (November 1958), 402-10.

Tetreau, E. D., "Arizona's Farm Laborers," *Arizona Agric. Exp. Station Bulletin No. 163* (May 1939).

Turley, Frank J., "A History of Babbitt Brothers Trading Company Emphasizing its Economic Influence on Northern Arizona," unpub. M.A. thesis (educ.), Arizona State Teachers College, Flagstaff, 1939.

Ullman, Edward L., "Amenities as a Factor in Regional Growth," *Geographical Review,* 44 (January 1954), 119-32.

van Dresser, Peter, "Rootstock for a New Regionalism," *Landscape,* 10 (Fall 1960), 11-14.

Wagoner, J. J., "The History of the Cattle Industry in Southern Arizona, 1540–1940," unpub. M.A. thesis (hist.), University of Arizona, 1949.

Waldrip, William I., "New Mexico During the Civil War," unpub. M.A. thesis (hist.), University of New Mexico, 1950.

Walker, Charles S., "Causes of the Confederate Invasion of New Mexico," *New Mexico Historical Review,* 8 (April 1933), 76-97.

Walker, E. S. Johnny, "The Scope of Federal Defense-Related Activity in New Mexico," *New Mexico Business,* 19 (April 1966), 1-4.

Waltz, Waldo E., "Arizona: A State of New-Old Frontiers," in Thomas C. Donnelly, ed., *Rocky Mountain Politics,* Albuquerque: University of New Mexico Press, 1940, 252-91.

Wilson, Andrew W., "The Impact of an Exploding Population on a Semi-Developed State: The Case of Arizona," *Arizona Review of Business and Public Administration,* 11, No. 1 (January 1962), 5-9.

Wilson, Owen Meredith, "A History of the Denver and Rio Grande Project, 1870–1901," unpub. Ph.D. dissertation, University of California, Berkeley, 1942.

"Winter Tourism in Tucson," *Arizona Progress,* Phoenix: Valley National Bank, monthly bulletin, April 1967.

Wyllys, Rufus Kay, *Arizona, The History of a Frontier State,* Phoenix: Hobson & Herr, 1950.

On Localities

Alvis, Berry Newton, "History of Union County, New Mexico," *New Mexico Historical Review,* 22 (July 1947), 247-73.

Baldwin, P. M., "A Short History of the Mesilla Valley," *New Mexico Historical Review,* 13 (July 1938), 314-24.

Bodine, John J., "The Tri-Ethnic Trap: The Spanish Americans in Taos," in June Helm, ed., *Spanish-Speaking People in the United States,* Seattle: American Ethnological Society, distributed by University of Washington Press, 1968, 145-53.

Boyle, Lucille, "The Economic History of Albuquerque, 1880–1893," unpub. M.A. thesis, University of New Mexico, 1948.

Burma, John H. and David E. Williams, "An Economic Social and Educational Survey of Rio Arriba and Taos Counties Prepared for Northern New Mexico College," mimeo (n.d. [1960's]), on file, Library, New Mexico Highlands University.

Choate, Edward Burleson, "History of the Capitan Community, 1890–1950," unpub. M.A. thesis (lib. arts), Eastern New Mexico University, 1954.

Conway, A. W., "A Northern New Mexico House Type," *Landscape,* 1 (Autumn 1951), 20-21.

Cummins, Densil Highfill, "Social and Economic History of Southwestern Colorado, 1860–1948," unpub. Ph.D. dissertation (hist.), University of Texas, 1951.

D'Antonio, William V. and William H. Form, *Influentials in two Border Cities, A Study in Community Decision-Making* [El Paso—Ciudad Juarez], South Bend: University of Notre Dame Press, 1965.

de Borhegyi, Stephen F., "The Evolution of a Landscape" [Chimayo], *Landscape,* 4 (Summer 1954), 24-30.

Duke, Robert W., "Political History of San Juan County, New Mexico, 1876–1926," unpub. M.A. thesis (hist.), University of New Mexico, 1947.

Fuchs, James R., "A History of Williams, Arizona 1876–1951," unpub. M.A. thesis (hist.), University of Arizona, 1952.

Grubbs, Frank H., "Frank Bond: Gentleman Sheepherder of Northern New Mexico, 1883–1915," *New Mexico Historical Review,* 35 (July and October 1960), 169-99, 293-308; 36 (April, July, and October 1961), 138-58, 230-43, 274-346; 37 (January 1962), 43-71.

Harding, J. W., "An Economic History of Harding County, New Mexico," unpub. M.A. thesis, New Mexico Normal University, 1933.

Hecht, Melvin E., "Folk Landscaping in the Southwestern Spanish Borderlands," Ms. obtained from the author.

History of Torrance County New Mexico, special edition of *The Daily Express,* Estancia, New Mexico, April 24, 1959.

Hoflich, Harold T. and T. J. McCleneghan, "Arizona's New Pulp and Paper Industry," *Arizona Review of Business and Public Administration,* 12 (July-August 1963), 1-8.

Horton, Arthur G., *An Economic, Political and Social Survey of Phoenix and the Valley of the Sun,* Tempe, Ariz.: Southside Progress, 1941.

Hurt, Wesley Robert, Jr., "Manzano: A Study of Community Disorganization," unpub. M.A. thesis (sociology), University of New Mexico, 1941.

Jeffrey, Robert S., "The History of Douglas, Arizona," unpub. M.A. thesis (hist.), University of Arizona, 1951.

Johnson, Bill Leslie, "An Ecological Study of Social Disorganization in Las Vegas, New Mexico," unpub. M.A. thesis (hist. and soc. sci.), New Mexico Highlands University, 1954.

Johanson, Sigurd and Milton Rossoff, "Community Planning in Eddy County, New Mexico," *New Mexico Agric. Exp. Station Bulletin No. 297* (December 1942).

Keleher, William A., *Maxwell Land Grant, A New Mexico Item,* New York: Argosy-Antiquarian Ltd., revised ed., 1964.

Kesel, Richard H., "The Raton Coal Field, An Evolving Landscape," *New Mexico Historical Review,* 41 (July 1966), 231-50.

Landgraf, John L., "Land-Use in the Ramah Area of New Mexico, An Anthropological Approach to Areal Study," *Papers of the Peabody Museum of American Archaeology and Ethnology,* Harvard University, 42 (1954).

Lange, Charles H., *Cochiti, A New Mexico Pueblo, Past and Present,* Austin: University of Texas Press, 1959.

Laumbach, Verna, "Las Vegas Before 1850," *New Mexico Historical Review,* 8 (October 1933), 241-64.

Leonard, Olen and C. P. Loomis, "Culture of a Contemporary Rural Community, El Cerrito, New Mexico," *Rural Life Studies No. 1,* U.S. Department of Agriculture, Bureau of Agricultural Economics (November 1941).

Loomis, Charles P., "El Cerrito, New Mexico: A Changing Village," *New Mexico Historical Review,* 33 (January 1958), 53-75.

Loomis, Charles P., "Ethnic Changes in the Southwest as Reflected in Two High Schools," *Sociometry,* 6 (February 1943), 7-26.

Loomis, Sylvia Glidden, ed., *Old Santa Fe Today,* Santa Fe: The School of American Research, 1966.

Lovell, Emily Kalled, *A Personalized History of Otero County, New Mexico,* Alamogordo: Star Pub. Co., 1963.

McCleneghan, Thomas J. and John H. Clark, "Mohave County—An Economy on the Upswing," *Arizona Review of Business and Public Administration,* 15 (February 1966), 10-17.

McCleneghan, T. J. and William L. Henderson, "A Look at the Developing Economy of Southeast Navajo County," *Arizona Review of Business and Public Administration,* 12 (November 1963), 1-10.

McConville, J. Lawrence, "A History of Population in the El Paso–Ciudad Juarez Area," unpub. M.A. thesis (Latin American studies), University of New Mexico, 1966.

McIntire, Elliot G., "Central Places on the Navajo Reservation, A Special Case," *Yearbook of the Association of Pacific Geographers,* 29 (1967), 91-96.

McIntire, Elliot G., "The Hopi Villages of Arizona: A Study in Changing Patterns," *Proceedings of the Association of American Geographers* 1 (1969), 95-99.

Morgan, Henry E., "A Brief History of Roosevelt County, New Mexico," unpub. M.A. thesis (hist.), University of New Mexico, 1938.

Morton, Dorothy Virginia, "A History of Quay County, New Mexico," unpub. M.A. thesis (hist.), University of Colorado, 1938.

Naegle, Conrad Keeler, "The History of Silver City, New Mexico 1870–1886," unpub. M.A. thesis (hist.), University of New Mexico, 1943.

Oberg, Kalervo, "Cultural Factors and Land-Use Planning in Cuba Valley, New Mexico," *Rural Sociology*, 5 (December 1940), 438-48.

Officer, James E., "Historical Factors in Inter-Ethnic Relations in the Community of Tucson," *Arizonian*, 1 (Fall 1960), 12-16.

Rebord, Bernice Ann, "A Social History of Albuquerque 1880–1885," unpub. M.A. thesis (hist.), University of New Mexico, 1947.

Robeson, Eva Jane, "The Mormon Exodus From Mexico in 1912 and the Subsequent Settlement in Southern New Mexico," unpub. M.A. thesis (hist.), New Mexico State University, 1960.

Rodgers, William M., "Historical Land Occupance of the Upper San Pedro River Valley Since 1870," unpub. M.A. thesis (geog. and area dev.), University of Arizona, 1965.

Rubright, Lynnell, "A Sequent Occupance of the Espanola Valley, New Mexico," unpub. M.A. thesis (geog.), University of Colorado, 1967.

Sasaki, Tom T., *Fruitland, New Mexico: A Navaho Community in Transition*, Ithaca: Cornell University Press, 1960.

Schultz, Vernon B., *Southwestern Town, The Story of Willcox, Arizona*, Tucson: University of Arizona Press, 1964.

Schweitzer, John L., "The Social Unity of Tucson's Chinese Community," unpub. M.A. thesis (anthro.), University of Arizona, 1952.

Scott, Winfield Townley, "The Still Young Sunlight, Chimayo, New Mexico," in Thomas C. Wheeler, ed., *A Vanishing America, The Life and Times of the Small Town*, New York: Holt, Rhinehart and Winston, 1964, 122-35.

Shinkle, James D., *Fifty Years of Roswell History—1867–1917*, Roswell: Hall-Poorbaugh Press, Inc., 1964.

Shock, Donald Paul, "The History of Flagstaff," unpub. M.A. thesis (hist.), University of Arizona, 1952.

Stanley, F., *The San Miguel del Bado New Mexico Story*, Pep, Texas: F. Stanley, 1964.

Stevens, Robert Conway, "A History of Chandler, Arizona, 1912–1953," unpub. M.A. thesis (hist.), University of Arizona, 1954.

Stone, Robert C., Frank A. Petroni, and Thomas J. McCleneghan, "Ambos

Nogales: Bi-Cultural Urbanism in a Developing Region," *Arizona Review of Business and Public Administration,* 12 (Jan. 1963), 1-31.

Stone, Robert C., et al., "Eloy: A Cotton Town in Transition," *Arizona Review of Business and Public Administration,* 9 (July–December 1960), in 4 sections.

Stone, Robert C. and Thomas T. McCleneghan, "Sierra Vista, Arizona, Urban Challenge in a Yearling Community," *Arizona Review of Business and Public Administration,* 8 (July and August 1959), 1-19, 1-11.

Tapy, Audrey Thomas, "Las Vegas 1890–1900, A Frontier Town Becomes Cosmopolitan," unpub. M.A. thesis (hist.), University of New Mexico, 1943.

Taylor, Morris F., *Trinidad, Colorado Territory,* Pueblo: O'Brien Printing & Stationery Co. and Trinidad State Junior College, 1966.

Thompson, Mrs. Harry and William H. Halley, *History of Clayton and Union County, New Mexico,* Denver: Monitor Pub. Co., 1962.

Twitchell, Ralph Emerson, *Old Santa Fe,* Santa Fe: Santa Fe New Mexican Pub. Co., 1925.

Vogt, Evon A. and Ethel M. Albert, eds., *People of Rimrock, A Study of Values in Five Cultures,* Cambridge: Harvard University Press, 1966.

Vogt, Evon Z., *Modern Homesteaders, The Life of a Twentieth-Century Frontier Community,* Cambridge: The Belknap Press of Harvard University Press, 1955.

Wadleigh, A. B., "Ranching in New Mexico, 1886–90" [Magdalena], *New Mexico Historical Review,* 27 (January 1952), 1-28.

Welch, Vernon E., "Las Vegas and the Adjacent Area During the Mexican Period," unpub. M.A. thesis, New Mexico Highlands University, 1950.

Westphall, Victor, "History of Albuquerque 1870–1880," unpub. M.A. thesis (hist.), University of New Mexico, 1947.

Widdison, Jerold Gwayn, "Historical Geography of the Middle Rio Puerco Valley, New Mexico," *New Mexico Historical Review,* 34 (October 1959), 248-84.

Yancy, James Walter, "The Negro of Tucson, Past and Present," unpub. M.A. thesis, University of Arizona, 1933.

INDEX

Phoenix, general regional position, 7, 80-81, 123; founding of, 43; Mormons near, 44; railroads, 45, 78; in 1900, 50-51; Anglos, 56; capital, 62-63; commerce and industry, 74-81; air service, 81, 125; growth, 85, 86; Negroes, 87, 93, 133; population, 88; in 1970, 105.

Pie Town, 70

Pima Indians, 15, 16, 36, 43, 55, 60, 61, 106, 112-13, 128

Pimeria Alta, 15

Piro pueblos, 31

Plantsite, 111

political geography
  political areas and social geography, 7, 62-64, 130; formation of American territories, 20-22; Gadsden Purchase, 22-23; agitation for new territories, 23-24; alteration of boundaries, 25-26; statehood issues, 89-90.

political parties, 50, 64, 90-93

populations (numbers)
  Indians, 10, 13, 31, 88; Hispanos, 14, 31; Southwest in 1900, 53, 64; Southwest in 1970, 82, 85-86; Negroes, 87; Orientals, 87; "Mexican stock," 88.

Prescott, 42, 45, 51, 78, 117

Pueblo, Colorado, 103, 117, 125

Puerto de Luna, 33

Pueblo Indians, 9-16, 23, 31, 34-35, 55, 59, 88-89, 99-101, 116, 128-29

Puerto Penasco, 80

Purgatoire River, 33

Railroads
  network, 45, 77-79; *Arizona Narrow-Guage*, 50; *Atchison, Topeka, and Santa Fe*, 39-40, 42, 45, 46, 51, 62, 76, 77, 79; *Atlantic and Pacific*, 26, 40, 42, 44, 51; *Chicago, Rock Island, and Pacific*, 77; *Denver and Rio Grande*, 38, 40, 46, 63; *El Paso and Southwestern*, 78-79; *Santa Fe Central*, 78; *Southern Pacific*, 40, 63, 77, 79; *Texas and Pacific*, 61.

Ramah, 118-19

Raton, 61

Raton Pass, 39, 40, 125

Rio Abajo, 12, 23, 27, 30, 32, 34, 97, 98

Rio Alamosa, 32

Rio Arriba, 12, 25, 27, 30, 34, 40, 47, 83, 91, 93, 101-3, 125

Rio Grande (basin, river, and valley)
  nuclear area, 7, 26, 120; Spanish conquest and occupation, 9-14; Santa Fe Trail, 18; political boundaries, 20-22; shift of channel, 32; Anglo foothold, 44; dam, 70; settlement along, 98-99.

Rio Mimbres, 34

Rio Puerco, 34, 97

Roosevelt Dam, 71

Roswell, 61, 74, 78, 81, 86, 126

Roy, 69

Ruidoso, 33

Sacaton, 55

Sacramento Mountains, 126

Saint David, 44

Saint Louis, Missouri, 19

Saint Michaels, 115

Salt Lake City, 6, 57

Salt River Valley, 35, 43, 44, 51, 71, 85, 105

San Antonio, Texas, 133

San Augustin Plains, 34

San Elizario, 110

San Francisco, California, 52

San Jose, Arizona, 60

San Jose River, 34, 35

San Juan (basin and river), 34, 36, 44, 45, 62, 73-74, 97, 124

San Juan de los Caballeros, 11

San Luis Valley, 25, 32, 34, 35, 40

San Manuel, 73

San Marcial, 32

San Miguel del Bado, 14, 18, 30

San Pedro Valley, 23, 31, 44, 112

San Xavier (del Bac), 32, 60

Sandia pueblo, 13, 98-99

Sandia range, 98

Santa Cruz (river and valley), 14, 23, 31, 35, 50, 60, 79, 112, 120